01603 773114
email: tis@ccn.ac.uk

NO
PARKING
LOADING ZONE
12 NOON TO 1 AM

CHARLIE TROTTER'S

DESSERTS

Recipes by
Charlie Trotter & Michelle Gayer

Wine Notes by
Brian Cronin

Color Photography by
Tim Turner

Black & White Photography by
Paul Elledge

Ten Speed Press, Berkeley, California

Contents

I'm a great believer in luck, and I find that the harder I work, the more I have of it. — Thomas Jefferson

Introduction

I have always considered desserts to be of equal importance
to the savory food, primarily because I think of the composi-
tion of the meal as a whole rather than in terms of individual
movements. I usually make dessert preparations in slightly
smaller portion sizes and serve more than just one. The desserts
profiled in these pages come right from the daily repertoire
at Charlie Trotter's, but they are far from signature dishes or
house specialties.

On any given day ten to fourteen different items are prepared and served, with each guest receiving between two and five desserts, depending on the dynamic of the dining experience, which evolves from the diners' moods, appetites, and wine selections, and even from the kitchen team's level of exuberance. Sometimes dramatic results can be achieved when you sieze control of a table of diners and give them far more than they ever dreamed.

I have long thought of the food at the restaurant as vegetable-driven cuisine where, besides outright vegetarian dishes, the preparations derive much of their identity and character from a liberal use of vegetables, herbs, and grains. As more than mere support items, vegetable elements provide extraordinary notes of depth and complexity, even for relatively simple preparations. I suppose it boils down to preserving pure, clean, explosive flavors—flavors that maintain their integrity and elegance. In the same way, my approach to desserts celebrates a fruit-driven style, where flash and visual pyrotechnics are shunned in favor of celebrating the glorious flavors of a perfectly ripe piece of fruit in the height of its season. After all, how does one improve on the perfection of tree-ripened, flawless peaches or apricots? We can only hope to step aside and let them sing.

Keep in mind when preparing these recipes, or any recipes for that matter, they are often meant to be used as a guide. And therein lies the beauty of all food—it is easy to change, adjust, and adapt as the foodstuffs dictate or your mood changes.

Certainly baking and pastry recipes require more exacting adherence than savory recipes, but there is still a fair amount of latitude to be spontaneous. This is particularly true with regards to substitution of ingredients, quantities served, and presentation. Although a tart dough recipe should be followed carefully, the filling, the size, and the shape of the tart are completely flexible. As for mistakes…don't worry! I have made plenty, but I always learn from my failures. In fact, I would say I have learned more from my failures than from my successes. James Joyce once remarked, "A person's errors are his portals of discovery." This is utterly true with regard to cuisine. So don't get frustrated, for you will surely learn more and more as you go.

As far as I'm concerned, a meal is not complete without a sweet thing or two at the end. Maybe it's simply a perfect fig or a bowl of luscious berries, or maybe it's a bittersweet burnt crème caramel, or a fraise des bois linzertorte or a jasmine rice pudding or tamarind soup with vanilla yogurt sorbet, or deep-dish apple pie with aged Cheddar cheese, or chocolate-cherry cake with cherry-cognac ice cream, or….

The reward of all action is to be found in enlightenment. — BHAGAVAD GITA

Soups & Sorbets

Fruit soups and sorbets are the most flavorful, yet simple, way of expressing the intricate flavors of fruit. The delicately sweet, refreshing characteristics of these early dessert preparations warrant equally sweet and refreshing wines. Effervescence is also prized in matching wines with these desserts because the silky texture of warm fruit soups seems to linger on the palate and begs to be cut with a little zing. The lightly sweet style of a Demi-Sec Champagne, or a delicate sparkling Muscat, such as Moscato d'Asti, is an elegant addition to such desserts. Crémant, a sparkling wine with less effervescence and a creamier texture than other sparklers, is also wonderful with these courses. Schramsberg Vineyards makes an exemplary Crémant that has just enough sweetness to be perfect. The vibrancy of the soup and sorbet with these wines will awaken your palate, preparing it for the more assertive flavors in later dessert courses.

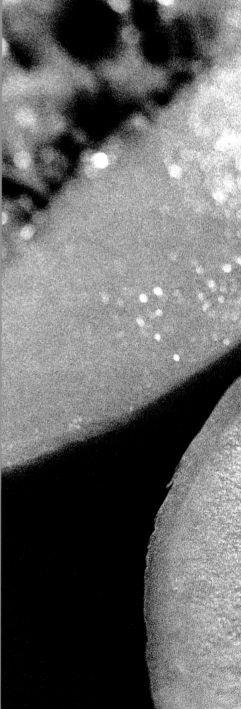

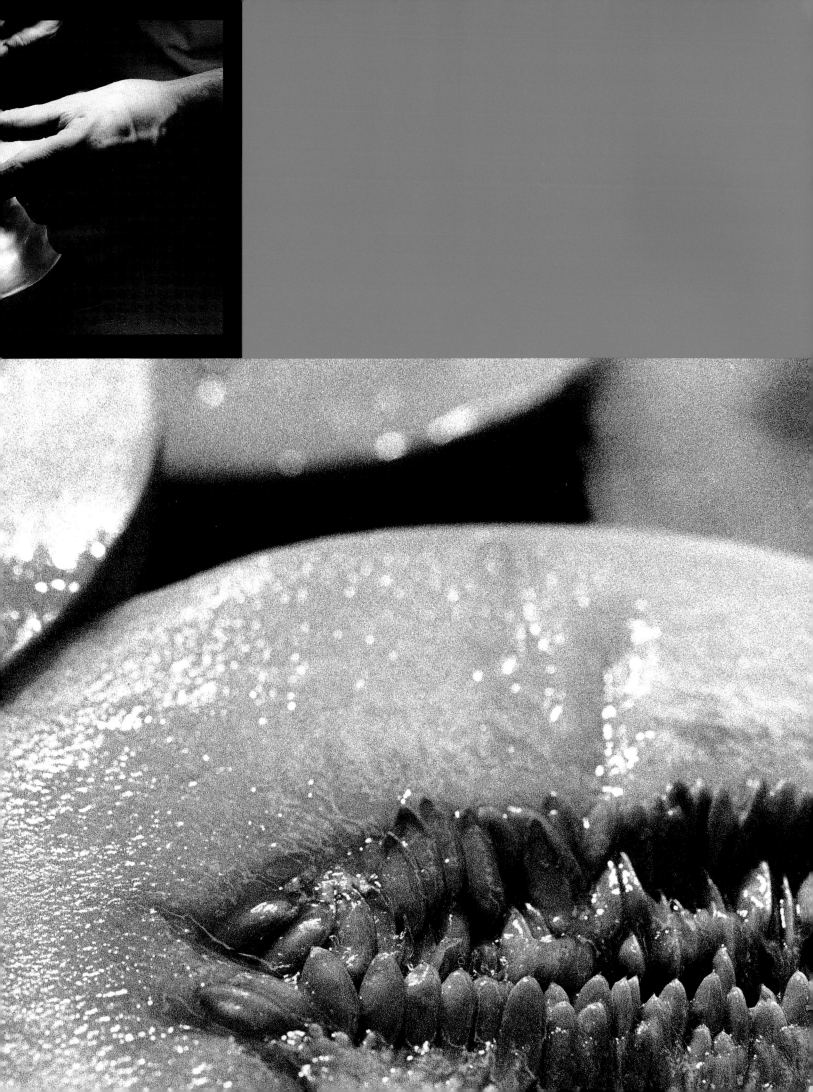

Lemongrass-Infused Indian Red Peach "Consommé" with Peach Sherbet

This peach soup takes on a haunting elegance with the addition of the lemongrass.
The various berries and cherries strewn about the bowl not only add further delectable flavors
but lend some truly exciting textural notes as well. The Peach Sherbet provides a seductive
smoothness that helps to meld all the textures and flavors into one,
while the crispy filo adds a playful element.

Serves 4.

6 Indian red peaches, peeled and chopped
²/₃ cup freshly squeezed orange juice
1 stalk lemongrass, chopped
²/₃ cup Simple Syrup (see Appendices)
1 Indian red peach, thinly sliced, skin on
¼ cup green gooseberries, cut in half
¼ cup golden gooseberries, cut in half
¼ cup red currants
¼ cup black currants
¼ cup Rainier cherries, pitted and quartered
¼ cup fresh blueberries
1 tablespoon tiny fresh thyme leaves
Filo Sticks (recipe follows)
Peach Sherbet (recipe follows)

METHOD To make the consommé: Purée the peaches, orange juice, lemongrass, and Simple Syrup for 2 minutes, or until smooth. Place in a cheesecloth-lined sieve over a bowl and refrigerate for approximately 3 hours, or until completely drained. It should yield about 3 cups of consommé.

ASSEMBLY Distribute the fruit evenly among 4 bowls and pour in some of the consommé. Sprinkle the thyme leaves around the bowls. Place 2 filo sticks across the bowls and top with 2 small scoops of Peach Sherbet.

Filo Sticks

Yield: about 50 sticks

3 sheets filo dough
¼ cup unsalted butter, melted
Confectioners' sugar, for dusting

METHOD Lay out a sheet of filo, brush with one-third of the butter, and sprinkle with confectioners' sugar. Top with another sheet of filo, brush with another third of the butter, and sprinkle with confectioners' sugar. Top with a final sheet of filo, brush with the remaining butter, and cut into ¼-inch-wide strips. (The extras allow for breakage.) Place the strips on a parchment-lined sheet pan and refrigerate for 30 minutes. Bake at 350 degrees for 15 minutes, or until golden brown. Cool and sprinkle with confectioners' sugar.

Peach Sherbet

Yield: approximately 1 quart

5 white peaches, peeled and chopped
³/₄ cup Simple Syrup (see Appendices)
¼ cup freshly squeezed lemon juice
1 cup milk

METHOD Purée the peaches, Simple Syrup, and lemon juice for 2 minutes or until smooth. Strain through a fine-mesh sieve and add the milk. Chill in the refrigerator, and then freeze in an ice cream machine. Keep frozen until ready to use.

Two Watermelon Soups with Frozen Yogurt Soufflé and Chocolate "Seeds"

This playful dish is quite refreshing in flavor and, in spite of its dramatic appearance, it is very easy to prepare. The two-toned effect is obtained by pouring the two soups into the bowl simultaneously; it's as easy as that. An ethereal frozen yogurt soufflé is placed in the center of the bowl to provide a sensual creaminess. The soufflé is topped with honeydew melon to further highlight the melon theme. Chocolate "seeds" are strewn about for a whimsical feeling. The great part about this dessert is that all the preparation is done well in advance and then it is plated at the last moment. To simplify, you could use a single soup.

Serves 8

3 cups chopped seedless golden or yellow watermelon

1 cup Simple Syrup (see Appendices)

1/2 cup freshly squeezed lemon juice

3 cups chopped seedless red watermelon

1 3/4 cups plus 2 tablespoons sugar

1 tablespoon water

1 tablespoon corn syrup

3 egg whites

1/2 cup heavy cream

1 cup plain yogurt

1 ounce bittersweet chocolate, tempered

1/2 cup finely diced honeydew melon

METHOD To make the soup: Purée the golden watermelon, 1/2 cup of the Simple Syrup, and 1/4 cup of the lemon juice for 3 minutes and strain through a fine-mesh sieve. Repeat the process with the red watermelon. Refrigerate the soups in separate small pitchers.

To make the frozen yogurt soufflé: Cook 3/4 cup plus 2 tablespoons of the sugar, the water, and corn syrup to the soft ball stage (230 degrees). Slowly whip the egg whites to soft peaks with an electric mixer on medium speed. Turn the mixer to high and slowly pour the sugar mixture down the side of the bowl. Whip until cool to the touch. Whisk together the cream and the remaining 1 cup of sugar and fold in the egg whites and yogurt. Pour into an 8 by 8-inch pan lined with plastic wrap and freeze. Cut out eight cylinders, using a 1½-inch round cutter, just prior to serving.

To make the chocolate seeds: Place small dots of the melted chocolate, the size of watermelon seeds, on a chilled, parchment-lined sheet pan. Using the tip of a paring knife, make a small tail at the base of the dots. Refrigerate until ready to use.

ASSEMBLY Simultaneously pour equal amounts of each soup into opposite sides of an individual bowl. Top each soufflé with some of the honeydew and place in the center of the bowl. Place several chocolate seeds around the bowl. Repeat with the remaining bowls. Serve just as the soufflé is beginning to soften.

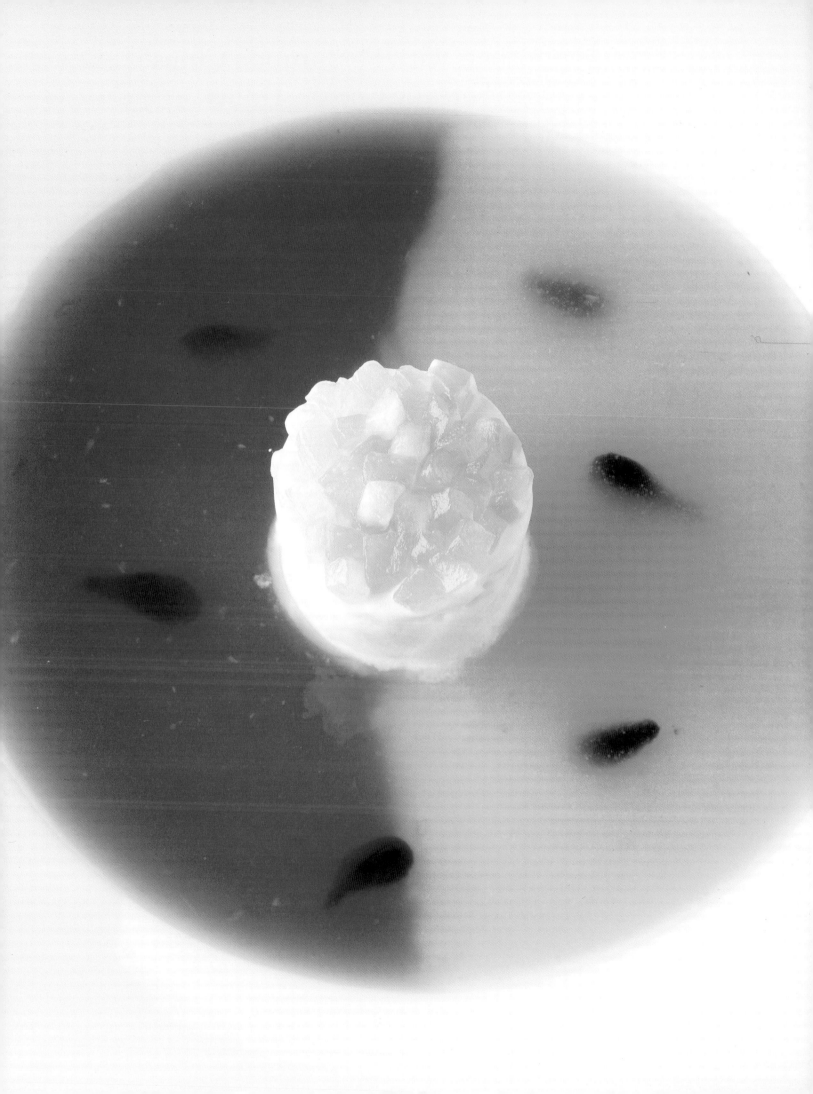

Tea Sorbets with Persimmon Chips
and Fortune Cookie Tuiles

*You don't need to stack these sorbets to achieve the full effect of their flavors;
it's merely a way to be a little playful with the presentation. The tea sorbets benefit nicely
from both the almond flavor in the Fortune Cookie Tuiles and the clean fruitiness
of the Persimmon Chips, and they also provide a welcome crunchiness.
This dessert is a wonderful, light way to end an Asian-themed meal.*

Serves 6

2 very ripe persimmons, skin and seeds removed

1 egg white

Green Tea Sorbet (recipe follows)

Fortune Cookie Tuiles (recipe follows)

Darjeeling Tea Sorbet (recipe follows)

Chamomile Tea Sorbet (recipe follows)

METHOD To make the Persimmon Chips: Cut the persimmons in quarters and purée with the egg white for 1 minute, or until smooth. Using an offset spatula, spread the batter into at least 30 small circles on a Silpat-lined or nonstick sheet pan. Bake at 225 degrees for 45 minutes, or until dry. Remove the chips from the pan while still warm and let cool on the counter or another flat surface.

ASSEMBLY Place a quenelle of Green Tea Sorbet in the center of each plate and top with a Fortune Cookie Tuile. Place a quenelle of Darjeeling Tea Sorbet on the tuiles and top with another tuile. Place a quenelle of Chamomile Tea Sorbet on top of the tuiles and press 5 persimmon chips vertically into the top of the quenelles of sorbet.

Green Tea Sorbet

Yield: 2 cups

1 cup freshly squeezed orange juice
1/2 cup sugar
2 tablespoons green tea

2 mangos, peeled and chopped
1/4 cup corn syrup

METHOD Bring the orange juice, sugar, and tea to a boil in a small saucepan. Cover, remove from heat, and steep for 30 minutes. Place in the blender with the remaining ingredients and purée for 2 minutes, or until smooth. Strain through a fine-mesh sieve, refrigerate to chill, and then freeze in an ice cream machine. Keep frozen until ready to use.

Fortune Cookie Tuiles

Yield: approximately 20 tuiles

3/4 cup plus 2 tablespoons flour
1/2 cup plus 2 tablespoons sugar
3 egg whites
2 tablespoons hot melted unsalted butter
1/2 teaspoon pure vanilla extract
3/4 teaspoon ground ginger

METHOD Combine the flour and sugar. Add the egg whites and combine on low speed in an electric mixer fitted with the paddle attachment. Add the melted butter in a steady stream and mix until incorporated. Add the vanilla and ginger and mix until combined. Cover with plastic wrap and refrigerate for at least 2 hours. Drop 1 teaspoon of the chilled batter onto a Silpat-lined or nonstick sheet pan and use an offset spatula to spread the batter into a 3-inch circle. Repeat with the remaining batter. Bake at 325 degrees for 7 to 10 minutes, or until light golden brown. Remove the tuiles from the pan while still warm and let cool on the counter or another flat surface.

Darjeeling Tea Sorbet

Yield: 1 1/2 cups

1 1/2 cups peeled, cored, and chopped ripe pears
1/2 cup water
1/2 cup freshly squeezed lemon juice
2 tablespoons Darjeeling tea, in a cheesecloth sachet
1/2 cup Simple Syrup (see Appendices)
2 tablespoons corn syrup

METHOD Bring the pears, water, and lemon juice to a boil. Add the tea, cover, remove from the heat, and steep for 30 minutes. Remove the sachet, squeezing out any liquid into the pan. Cool the mixture slightly, then purée with the Simple Syrup and corn syrup for 2 minutes, or until smooth. Strain through a fine-mesh sieve, refrigerate to chill, and then freeze in an ice cream machine. Keep frozen until ready to use.

Chamomile Tea Sorbet

Yield: 1 1/2 cups

1 1/2 cups apple juice
1/4 cup freshly squeezed lime juice
2 tablespoons chamomile tea
1 tablespoon corn syrup
1/4 cup Simple Syrup (see Appendices)

METHOD Bring the apple and lime juices to a boil. Add the tea, cover, and steep for 30 minutes. Strain through a fine-mesh sieve and then stir in the corn syrup and Simple Syrup. Refrigerate to chill and then freeze in an ice cream machine. Keep frozen until ready to use.

Horned Melon and Persimmon Granités with Shaved Persimmon, Cactus Pear, and Sapote

When a granité is made properly, it is a delicate, shaved ice that melts instantly in your mouth and simultaneously explodes with the flavor of the fruit used in it. Granités are very easy to make— ripe seasonal fruit, simple syrup, and some citrus are all that is required. A granité makes a wonderful prelude to something more substantial, like a warm fruit or chocolate dessert, or it can stand alone as a healthful, light choice that is more interesting than just a plate of fruit. I always like to pair a fruit granité with slices or pieces of the respective fruit used in making it for an added textural dimension and to fabulously enhance the flavor of the fruit. Here, the combination of horned melon (or any other type of melon), persimmons, and cactus pear is both luscious and exotic.

Serves 6

2 cactus pears

¼ cup Simple Syrup (See Appendices)

1½ teaspoons freshly squeezed lime juice

¾ cup very thinly sliced ripe persimmon

¾ cup very thinly sliced cactus pear

¾ cup very thinly sliced sapote

Persimmon Granité (recipe follows)

Horned Melon Granité (recipe follows)

METHOD To make the sauce: Cut the cactus pears in half. Hold the pears with a towel to protect your hands from the prickly needles and scoop out the pulp. Purée the cactus pear pulp with the Simple Syrup and lime juice for 1 minute, or until smooth. Strain through a fine-mesh sieve.

ASSEMBLY Place 2 or 3 slices of the persimmon in the center of each plate. Top with the cactus pear and sapote slices. Repeat the process, creating 2 layers of each fruit. Place a small spoonful of Persimmon Granité on the fruit and top with a small spoonful of Horned Melon Granité. Repeat, creating 2 layers of each granité. Drizzle the cactus pear sauce around the plate.

Persimmon Granité

Yield: 1 quart

3 small ripe persimmons, peeled and chopped

½ cup Simple Syrup (see Appendices)

⅓ cup freshly squeezed orange juice

¼ cup water

METHOD Combine all of the ingredients in a blender and purée for 2 minutes, or until smooth. Strain through a fine-mesh sieve, pour into a shallow pan, and freeze. To form the granité, scrape the mixture with a spoon every 15 to 20 minutes for 2 hours, or until frozen.

Horned Melon Granité

Yield: 1 quart

3 horned melons, quartered and pulp scraped out

3 tablespoons freshly squeezed lime juice

½ to ¾ cup Simple Syrup (see Appendices)

METHOD Combine the melon, lime juice, and ½ cup Simple Syrup in a blender and purée for 2 minutes, or until smooth. Add the additional Simple Syrup to taste. Strain through a fine-mesh sieve, pour into a shallow pan, and freeze. To form the granité, scrape the mixture with a spoon every 15 to 20 minutes for 2 hours, or until frozen.

Granny Smith Apple Fritter
with Apple Cider Soup

This is a great way to enjoy the purity of the flavor of Granny Smith apples.
The crispy, fried fritter belies the refined, simple beauty of the soup, and a meaty piece
of poached apple bridges the two disparate components. Much of this dish can be prepared
in advance because only the fritter has to be made at the last minute. A scoop of vanilla ice cream
can be placed on top of the fritter to add richness and a wonderful temperature contrast.

Serves 6

6 cups apple cider

1 cinnamon stick

1/2 cup sugar

3 tablespoons freshly squeezed lemon juice

1 tablespoon orange zest

2 whole allspice berries

2 Granny Smith apples, peeled and cored

1 cup white wine

1/2 cup honey

1/4 teaspoon freshly grated nutmeg

Apple Fritters (recipe follows)

METHOD To make the soup: Cook the apple cider, cinnamon stick, sugar, lemon juice, orange zest, and allspice over medium heat for 30 minutes, or until reduced by half. Strain through a fine-mesh sieve. Warm before serving.

To make the apple rings: Cut each apple crosswise into three 1/4-inch-thick slices. Bring the white wine, honey, and nutmeg to a boil. Add the apple slices and simmer for 15 minutes, or until tender. Set aside in the poaching liquid and warm before serving.

ASSEMBLY Place a warm poached apple slice in the center of each bowl. Pour in some of the warm soup and place an Apple Fritter on top of the apple slices.

Apple Fritters

Yield: 12 to 15 fritters

1/2 cup plus 2 tablespoons bread flour

1/4 teaspoon salt

1 egg, separated

3 tablespoons granulated sugar

1/2 teaspoon finely chopped lemon zest

1/2 cup sweet white wine

Pulp of 1 vanilla bean

2 apples, peeled and cut in 1/8-inch julienne

Oil, for deep-frying

Confectioners' sugar, for dusting

METHOD Sift together the flour and salt. Mix the egg yolk, 1 1/2 tablespoons of the granulated sugar, and the lemon zest in a separate bowl until just combined. Add the wine and vanilla to the egg mixture and stir the mixture into the flour until completely smooth. Refrigerate for 30 minutes. Just before serving, whip the egg white until foamy. Slowly add the remaining 1 1/2 tablespoons granulated sugar and continue whipping until stiff peaks form. Fold the egg whites and julienned apples into the batter until just combined.

Heat the oil over medium-high heat. Using a fork, lift some of the batter from the bowl and drop it into the hot oil. Cook the fritter for 2 minutes on each side, or until golden brown. Remove to paper towels to drain, let cool slightly, and dust with confectioners' sugar.

Trio of Sorbets with Pomegranate Seeds and Guava Purée

Serving sorbets with a smooth, rich purée makes them taste creamier. Here, four distinct but complementary flavors blend and play off each other brilliantly: almond, passion fruit, vanilla yogurt and guava are woven in seamless, tropical harmony. Citrus segments and pomegranate seeds add further textural complexity, and the Oven-Dried Pineapple Chips provide a delightful cleanliness. This dish could easily be turned into a soup by thinning out the guava purée.

Serves 6

3 pineapple guavas
¼ cup Simple Syrup (see Appendices)
1 tablespoon water
¾ cup unsweetened pineapple juice
12 Satsuma orange segments
⅓ cup peeled and diced strawberry papaya
⅓ cup peeled and diced pineapple guava
½ cup pomegranate seeds
Vanilla Yogurt Sorbet (recipe follows)
Passion Fruit Sorbet (recipe follows)
Almond Milk Sherbet (recipe follows)
Oven-Dried Pineapple Chips (recipe follows)

METHOD To make the guava purée: Peel the pineapple guavas and purée with the Simple Syrup and water for 2 minutes, or until smooth. Strain through a fine-mesh sieve.

ASSEMBLY Drizzle 1 tablespoon of the guava purée and 2 tablespoons of the pineapple juice around each bowl. Arrange 2 orange segments and some of the diced papaya, guava, and some of the pomegranate seeds around each bowl. Place a quenelle of each of the 3 sorbets in the center of the bowls and insert a Pineapple Chip upright in the center of each quenelle.

Vanilla Yogurt Sorbet

Yield: approximately 1 quart

½ cup Vanilla Simple Syrup (see Appendices)
Pulp of 1 vanilla bean
3 cups plain yogurt

METHOD Warm the Vanilla Simple Syrup with the vanilla pulp and refrigerate to chill. Add the yogurt and freeze in an ice cream machine. Keep frozen until ready to use.

Passion Fruit Sorbet

Yield: approximately 1 pint

12 passion fruit
⅓ cup Simple Syrup (see Appendices)
¾ cup freshly squeezed orange juice
2 tablespoons corn syrup

METHOD Cut the passion fruit in half and scoop the pulp into a blender. Blend for 15 seconds and strain through a fine-mesh sieve. Discard the seeds. Combine the passion fruit with the remaining ingredients, refrigerate to chill, and then freeze in an ice cream machine. Keep frozen until ready to use.

Almond Milk Sherbet

Yield: approximately 1 quart

4 cups milk
1 pound almonds, lightly toasted and chopped
¼ cup corn syrup
¼ cup Simple Syrup (see Appendices)
Pinch of salt

METHOD Bring the milk and almonds to a boil. Lower the heat and simmer for 30 minutes. Cover and remove from heat to cool. Purée for 2 minutes, or until smooth, and refrigerate overnight. Strain through a fine-mesh sieve. Add the corn syrup, Simple Syrup, and salt and freeze in an ice cream machine. Keep frozen until ready to use.

Oven-Dried Pineapple Chips

Yield: 18 chips

18 ¹⁄₁₆-inch-thick slices of pineapple
2 teaspoons sugar

METHOD Lay the pineapple slices on a Silpat-lined or nonstick sheet pan. Sprinkle lightly with the sugar and bake at 225 degrees for 75 to 90 minutes, or until dry and light golden brown. Remove from the pan while warm, set aside to cool completely, and store in an airtight container at room temperature until ready to use.

Sorbet Terrine with French Melon Soup

While it looks quite complex, making a sorbet or ice cream terrine is simple to do once the sorbets are made or bought. You merely smooth one layer of softened sorbet into a terrine mold and when it firms up a bit in the freezer, spread on the next layer. Any flavors that are compatible, such as melon and berry, will work. In this dessert, a multifruit sorbet terrine is served with some of the same fruits that make up the terrine in a smooth, lush soup. As an option, crème fraîche can be drizzled around the soup to provide an element of richness. The terrine can be sliced and laid in the bowl or, for a more enticing presentation, it can be cut into wedges and positioned upright.

Serves 6

2 to 3 French melons, peeled, seeded, and chopped (about 3 cups)

1 cup freshly squeezed orange juice

¼ cup freshly squeezed lime juice

½ cup Simple Syrup (see Appendices)

Pinch of salt

Bing Cherry Sorbet (recipe follows)

Ginger-Buttermilk Sherbet (recipe follows)

Strawberry Sorbet (recipe follows)

Peach Sorbet (recipe follows)

Rhubarb Sorbet (recipe follows)

¼ cup red fraises des bois, halved

¼ cup Bing cherries, pitted and quartered

1 peach, scooped into Parisienne balls

¼ cup Poached Rhubarb Strips (see Appendices)

¼ cup Preserved Ginger (see Appendices)

2 lemon balm leaves, julienned

2 tablespoons crème fraîche

METHOD To make the soup: Purée the French melon, orange juice, and lime juice for 3 minutes, or until smooth. Add the Simple Syrup and salt and strain through a fine-mesh sieve. Refrigerate until ready to use.

To make the terrine: Line a 1½ by 2¼ by 8-inch terrine mold with plastic wrap. Spread a ⅜-inch layer of Bing Cherry Sorbet in the bottom of the terrine mold and freeze for 30 minutes. Spread a layer of Ginger-Buttermilk Sherbet in the mold and freeze for 30 minutes. Continue the layering with the Strawberry Sorbet, and the Peach Sorbet, ending with the Rhubarb Sorbet; freeze for 30 minutes after adding each layer. Cut the terrine into ½-inch-thick slices and cut each slice in half diagonally.

ASSEMBLY Stand 3 triangles of the terrine in each bowl. Ladle some of the soup into each bowl. Strew the fraises des bois, cherries, peaches, Poached Rhubarb Strips, Preserved Ginger, and lemon balm around the bowl and drizzle with the crème fraîche.

Bing Cherry Sorbet

Yield: approximately 1 pint

30 Bing cherries, pitted
½ cup Simple Syrup (see Appendices)
⅔ cup freshly squeezed orange juice
¼ cup corn syrup

METHOD Purée the cherries, Simple Syrup, and orange juice for 3 minutes, or until smooth. Strain through a fine-mesh sieve and add the corn syrup. Place in the refrigerator to chill and then freeze in an ice cream machine. Keep frozen until ready to use.

Ginger-Buttermilk Sherbet

Yield: approximately 1 pint

3 tablespoons peeled and chopped fresh ginger
6 tablespoons Simple Syrup (see Appendices)
1½ cups buttermilk
2 tablespoons corn syrup

METHOD Purée the ginger and Simple Syrup for 3 minutes, or until smooth. Strain through a fine-mesh sieve and add the buttermilk and corn syrup. Chill and then freeze in an ice cream machine.

Strawberry Sorbet

Yield: approximately 1 pint

2 cups fresh strawberries
¼ cup freshly squeezed lemon juice
½ cup Simple Syrup (see Appendices)

METHOD Purée all of the ingredients for 3 minutes, or until smooth. Strain through a fine-mesh sieve, chill in a refrigerator, and then freeze in an ice cream machine. Keep frozen until ready to use.

Peach Sorbet

Yield: approximately 1 pint

4 peaches, peeled, pitted, and cut into chunks
¼ cup freshly squeezed lemon juice
½ cup Simple Syrup (see Appendices)
¼ cup water

METHOD Bring all of the ingredients to a boil and then simmer for 3 minutes. Purée for 3 minutes, or until smooth, and strain through a fine-mesh sieve. Chill in a refrigerator and then freeze in an ice cream machine. Keep frozen until ready to use.

Rhubarb Sorbet

Yield: 2 cups

4 stalks rhubarb, chopped (about 2½ cups)
½ cup Simple Syrup (see Appendices)
½ cup water

METHOD Bring all of the ingredients to a boil and then simmer for 5 minutes, or until the rhubarb is tender. Purée for 3 minutes, or until smooth, and strain through a fine-mesh sieve. Chill in a refrigerator and then freeze in an ice cream machine. Keep frozen until ready to use.

Apricot Soup with Lychee Nuts, Lychee Nut Ice Cream, and Caged Fruit Salad

*The combination of slightly astringent apricots and rich, luscious lychee nuts is terrifically
satisfying. In this preparation the lychee appears in two forms—raw and as an ice cream.
As the ice cream melts, it gradually tones the rather direct flavor of the apricot soup.
So, if you eat this dessert slowly, you will enjoy a range of gustatory experiences as the
flavor combinations literally develop between spoonfuls. The caged fruit salad adds
a stunning visual effect as well as more complexity of flavor, but it can easily be omitted
and the fruits can simply be strewn around the bowl.*

Serves 8

³/₄ cup sugar

¹/₄ cup water

6 apricots, pitted and coarsely chopped

*¹/₂ cup freshly squeezed orange juice,
warmed*

1 Friar plum, pitted and thinly sliced

1 apricot, pitted and thinly sliced

¹/₂ cup Black Corinth grapes

1 small carambola, thinly sliced

1 teaspoon finely julienned lemon verbena

24 lychee nuts, pitted and halved

Lychee Nut Ice Cream (recipe follows)

Sugar Cages (recipe follows)

METHOD To make the soup: Cook the sugar
and water in a small, heavy-bottomed sauté
pan over medium heat for 5 minutes, or
until lightly golden. Add the chopped apricots and stir until coated. Add the orange
juice, simmer for 2 to 3 minutes to dissolve
any hardened sugar, then remove from the
heat. Let the mixture cool slightly and then
purée in a blender for 3 minutes, or until
smooth. Strain through a fine-mesh sieve
and refrigerate until ready to use. Thin
with a little water if necessary.

To make the fruit salad: Toss together the
plum, sliced apricot, grapes, carambola, and
lemon verbena.

ASSEMBLY Arrange 6 lychee nut halves to
form a circle in the center of each bowl and
top with a Lychee Nut Ice Cream disc.
Place the Sugar Cages on the ice cream
discs and gently spoon some of the fruit
salad inside the cages. Ladle the soup into
the bowls and serve immediately.

Lychee Nut Ice Cream

Yield: approximately 3 cups

2 cups heavy cream

¹/₂ cup sugar

4 egg yolks

¹/₂ cup pitted lychee nuts

METHOD Prepare an ice water bath. Bring
the cream to a boil. Whisk together the
sugar and egg yolks and slowly pour in
some of the hot cream to temper the eggs.
Pour the egg mixture into the cream and
cook for 2 to 3 minutes, or until the mixture
coats the back of a spoon and steam rises
from the top. Cool the mixture over the ice
water bath, stirring occasionally, until
chilled. Purée the lychee nuts and the ice
cream base for 2 minutes, or until smooth.
Strain through a fine-mesh sieve and
freeze in an ice cream machine. Spread the

ice cream in an 8 by 8-inch pan lined with
plastic wrap. Place in the freezer for 1 hour,
or until frozen solid. Turn the ice cream out
of the pan, remove the plastic wrap, and cut
into 1¹/₂-inch discs.

Sugar Cages

Yield: 8 cages

1 cup sugar

¹/₄ cup water

2 tablespoons corn syrup

METHOD Combine all of the ingredients in
a heavy-bottomed sauté pan and cook over
medium heat for 10 minutes, or until amber
in color. Remove from the heat. Place a
piece of heavy-duty aluminum foil over the
outside of a 1-ounce ladle and lightly oil the
foil. Using a spoon, drizzle the sugar syrup
over the upside-down ladle, starting at 12
o'clock and ending at 6 o'clock, and repeat
the movement, creating a web of sugar
spokes that forms a cage. Run some sugar
syrup crosswise around the spokes to give
the cage stability. Let the sugar syrup cool
completely and then gently remove the foil
from the ladle, releasing the cage. Repeat
the process to make the remaining 7 cages.
(You may have to reheat the sugar slightly
between uses.)

Citrus Fruits

Citrus fruits can often be difficult to pair with wine because the acidity of the fruit dominates and hides the wonderful characteristics of most sweet wines. However, the fresh, young style of lightly fortified Muscats, with their orange-blossom aromas and delicate citrus flavors, achieves an incredible harmony with the fruit.  Wines such as Muscat Baume de Venise, Muscat de Rivesaltes, Muscat de Lunel, and other similar New World Muscats are good. Some New World late-harvest Rieslings can also be paired with these citrus desserts with equally good results. Try Mount Horrock's "Cordon Cut" Riesling from South Australia or Chateau St. Michelle's Late Harvest Riesling from Washington State's Columbia Valley. Lemon flavors and resounding acidity enable these wines to linger on the palate for what seems like forever.

Key Lime "Pie" with Carambola

~~~~~~

*This dessert is simply Key lime pie. The lime custard is baked on a sheet pan and then
cut into discs, or whatever shape is desired. Thin slices of carambola are baked into the custard
for an additional lush, tropical flavor, but practically any tropical fruit would
brilliantly accompany this smooth, elegant custard. The custard discs are layered with
crispy meringues to create an unlikely napoleon. Oven-dried slices of carambola
and a carambola sauce further accentuate the marvelous flavors in this dish.
For a more traditional approach this custard could easily be baked in a tart shell
and served with a carambola fruit salad.*

Serves 4

3 whole eggs

9 egg yolks

2 cups plus 2 tablespoons sugar

1 cup freshly squeezed Key lime juice

*2 small carambolas, cut in twelve
¼-inch-thick slices, seeds removed*

2 egg whites

Pinch of salt

4 Key limes

¼ cup Simple Syrup (see Appendices)

Oven-Dried Carambola (recipe follows)

Carambola Sauce (recipe follows)

1 tablespoon chopped Key lime zest

METHOD To make the custard: Cook the whole egg, egg yolks, 2 cups of the sugar, and the lime juice in a double boiler over barely simmering water, stirring continuously, for 5 minutes, or until thickened. Strain through a fine-mesh sieve. Lightly oil a 9 by 13-inch pan, line with plastic wrap, and pour in the custard. Trim off any brown edges on the tips of the carambola slices and evenly space them on top of the custard. Bake in a water bath at 325 degrees for 30 minutes, or until the custard is set. Cool and refrigerate until ready to use. Cut twelve 2-inch circles in the custard, making sure that there is a carambola slice in the center of each circle.

To make the meringue: Whip the egg whites until frothy, add the remaining 2 tablespoons of sugar and the salt and continue whipping until soft peaks form. Spoon the mixture into a pastry bag and pipe, or spread, into at least 8 circles 2 inches in diameter and ⅛ inch thick on a Silpat-lined or nonstick sheet pan. Bake at 200 degrees for 2 hours, or until thoroughly dry.

To prepare the limes: Cut the top and bottom off the 4 Key limes. Cut the peel and white pith from the limes and then cut on both sides of each membrane to release the fruit segments. Cook the lime segments in the Simple Syrup until warm.

ASSEMBLY Arrange 4 pieces of Oven-Dried Carambola in the center of each plate and place a custard circle on top. Place a meringue, another circle of custard, another meringue, and another circle of custard on the stacks. Arrange the lime segments around the plates. Spoon some of the Carambola Sauce around the limes and sprinkle the fruit with lime zest.

Oven-Dried Carambola

Yield: 16 to 20 slices

2 carambolas, cut into at least sixteen ¼-inch-thick slices, seeds removed

2 tablespoons sugar

METHOD Lay out the carambola on a Silpat-lined or nonstick sheet pan. Sprinkle with the sugar and bake at 225 degrees for 1 hour, or until dried. Remove from the pan and cool on a counter or another flat surface. Store in an airtight container until ready to use.

Carambola Sauce

Yield: approximately 1 cup

¼ cup sugar

2 tablespoons water

*2 carambolas, cut into chunks
(about 1½ to 2 cups)*

METHOD Cook the sugar and water in a small, heavy-bottomed sauté pan over medium heat for 5 minutes, or until light golden brown. Add the carambola and stir until completely coated. Cook over low heat for 2 to 3 minutes to dissolve all of the caramel and soften the fruit. Purée for 2 minutes, or until smooth, and strain through a fine-mesh sieve. Let cool to room temperature before serving.

Meyer Lemon Pudding Cake
with Persimmon and Tarragon Anglaise

*The Meyer lemon is splendidly showcased in this ethereal pudding cake, and the hint of tarragon
provides an unexpected, haunting flavor. Persimmons have a rich, tropical flavor that
works brilliantly with the refined tartness of the Meyer lemon. The pudding cake and the sauces
can be made up to a day in advance, making this a great dish to serve at a dinner party.
It can also be made with lime or orange juice for different, but equally pleasing, flavors.*

Serves 8

¼ cup unsalted butter

1¼ cups sugar

Pinch of salt

3 tablespoons Meyer lemon zest

6 egg yolks

6 tablespoons flour

½ cup freshly squeezed Meyer lemon juice

2 cups milk

8 egg whites

4 ripe persimmons, peeled

*2 tablespoons Simple Syrup, plus additional,
as needed (see Appendices)*

Tarragon Anglaise (recipe follows)

1 tablespoon julienned fresh tarragon

METHOD To make the pudding cakes: Cream the butter, 1 cup plus 2 tablespoons of the sugar, the salt, and lemon zest. Add the egg yolks one at a time, mixing well after each addition. Add the flour and mix well. Add ¼ cup of the lemon juice and the milk and mix until combined. Beat the egg whites to stiff peaks and fold into the batter.

Immediately pour the batter into a plastic wrap–lined 9 by 13-inch pan and bake in a water bath at 325 degrees for 35 to 45 minutes, or until golden brown and firm. Let cool and then invert onto a sheet pan and refrigerate to chill. Use a ring cutter to cut out eight 3-inch circles just prior to serving.

To prepare the persimmons: Slice 2 of the persimmons into ⅛-inch wedges and set aside.

To make the persimmon chips: Cut 1 of the persimmons in half lengthwise and then cut one of the halves into paper thin slices. Lay the slices on a Silpat-lined or nonstick sheet pan and sprinkle with 1 to 2 tablespoons of the sugar. Bake at 225 degrees for 45 minutes, or until dry. Remove the persimmon chips from the pan while still warm, twist slightly, and cool. Store in an airtight container until ready to use.

To make the persimmon sauce: Purée the remaining 1½ persimmons with the remaining ¼ cup lemon juice and the Simple Syrup for 2 minutes, or until smooth.

Strain through a fine-mesh sieve and thin with additional Simple Syrup, if necessary.

ASSEMBLY Place a circle of cake in the center of each plate and arrange the persimmon slices on top in a pinwheel. Drizzle the persimmon sauce and the Tarragon Anglaise around the plates and sprinkle with the julienned tarragon and persimmon chips.

Tarragon Anglaise

Yield: 1 cup

¾ cup plus 2 tablespoons heavy cream

2 sprigs tarragon

2 egg yolks

1 tablespoon sugar

METHOD Bring the cream and tarragon to a boil. Whisk together the egg yolks and sugar and slowly pour in some of the hot cream to temper the eggs. Pour the egg mixture into the cream and cook for 2 to 3 minutes, or until the mixture coats the back of a spoon and steam rises from the top. Just prior to serving, blend with a handheld blender until frothy.

Blood Orange Soufflé with Chocolate Sorbet

This rustic preparation is one of the simplest and most festive ways I know to present a soufflé and it's a great way to enjoy fruit and chocolate simultaneously. Oranges and chocolate are a classic combination, but blood oranges, with their slightly greater astringency than most oranges, make this pairing even more elegant. The warm orange peel provides a wonderful citrus perfume that entices the senses. The chocolate sorbet is clean and light, yet it has a powerful flavor. Blood orange segments enhance the enjoyment of the fruit flavors, and the crispy chocolate tuiles add just the right textural contrast.

Serves 6

10 blood oranges
½ cup milk
2 tablespoons unsalted butter
1 egg yolk
¾ cup sugar
¾ teaspoon cornstarch
¼ cup egg whites (about 2 egg whites)
¼ cup water
Chocolate Sorbet (see Appendices)
Chocolate Tuiles (recipe follows)

METHOD To prepare the oranges: Zest 2 of the blood oranges and set the zest aside. Cut the remaining peel off the 2 oranges and then cut on both sides of the membranes, reserving the orange segments. Squeeze out and reserve any juice in the membranes, and discard the membranes. Cut the tops off 6 of the blood oranges and use your fingers to remove the pulp, being careful not to pierce the skin. Turn the orange shells upside down to drain out any liquid. Squeeze the pulp, reserving the juice and add it to the juice from the membranes. Squeeze the juice from the remaining 2 oranges and add to the already reserved juice. (There should be 1½ to 2 cups of juice.)

To make the soufflé: Prepare an ice water bath. Bring the milk, butter, and half of the orange zest to a boil. Whisk together the egg yolk, 2 tablespoons of the sugar, and the cornstarch and slowly pour in some of the hot milk mixture to temper the egg yolks. Pour the egg yolks into the milk mixture and bring it back to a boil, whisking continuously. Strain through a fine-mesh sieve and cool over an ice water bath, stirring occasionally, until chilled.

Cook 1 cup of the blood orange juice with the remaining orange zest over medium-high heat for 15 minutes, or until reduced to ¼ cup. Strain the liquid through a fine-mesh sieve, cool, and mix into the milk mixture.

Whisk the egg whites until frothy, add 2 tablespoons of the sugar, and continue whisking until soft peaks form. Fold the blood orange juice mixture into the egg whites. Spoon the mixture into the 6 orange cups, filling each about three-quarters of the way full. Place the orange cups on a sheet pan and bake at 325 degrees for 10 to 15 minutes, or until lightly browned and set. Serve immediately.

To make the sauce: Cook the remaining ½ cup sugar and the water in a small, heavy-bottomed sauté pan over medium heat for 5 minutes, or until golden brown and caramelized. Add the remaining ½ to 1 cup orange juice and bring to a boil. Lower to medium-low heat, add the blood orange segments, and stir until completely coated. Keep warm until ready to serve.

ASSEMBLY Place an orange soufflé and some of the blood orange segments on each plate. Drizzle the orange-caramel sauce around the segments. Sandwich a quenelle of Chocolate Sorbet between 2 Chocolate Tuiles and place it next to the orange cup.

Chocolate Tuiles

Yield: 1½ cups batter

6 tablespoons unsalted butter
Pulp and pod of ½ vanilla bean
3 egg whites
½ cup plus 1 tablespoon sugar
¼ cup plus 1 tablespoon flour
¼ cup unsweetened cocoa

METHOD Melt the butter with the vanilla pulp and bean, remove from the heat, discard the vanilla bean, and let cool. Whisk the egg whites until frothy. Gradually add the sugar and whisk until soft peaks form. Mix in the cooled butter. Sift the flour and cocoa together in a separate bowl and fold in until just combined.

Drop ½ teaspoon of the batter onto a Silpat-lined or nonstick sheet pan and spread into a 2-inch circle using an offset spatula. Repeat this process, making at least 16 tuiles, to allow for breakage. (Extra batter can be refrigerated for up to 1 week.) Bake at 325 degrees for 5 to 8 minutes, or until set. Carefully remove the tuiles from the pan while they are still warm and cool on a counter or another flat surface. If the tuiles harden on the sheet pan, they can be returned to the oven to soften.

Ugli Fruit and Pink Grapefruit Gratin with Pink Grapefruit–Chile-Tequila Sorbet

This is a very cleansing, refreshing combination. The sorbet explodes with the clean, exciting flavors of jalepeño and tequila against the backdrop of soothing pink grapefruit, and the sabayon provides just the right amount of sating richness. This preparation can stand alone for a light conclusion to a meal or it can be a wonderful first course before something more substantial.

Serves 4

2 Ugli fruits

2 pink grapefruits

1/2 cup honey

Brioche Dough (see Appendices, but add zest of 1 lemon and 2 oranges with butter)

Vanilla Tuile Batter (see Appendices)

Crème Fraîche Sabayon (recipe follows)

Pink Grapefruit–Chile-Tequila Sorbet (recipe follows)

METHOD To prepare the fruit: Cut the peel and white pith off the Ugli fruit and grapefruits. Cut along both sides of each membrane to release the segments of fruit. Discard the membranes. Toss together the Ugli fruit, grapefruit, and honey and refrigerate for at least 1 hour.

To make the brioche: Place the dough in a parchment-lined, buttered 7½ by 3½-inch loaf pan (4½- to 5-cup capacity) and allow to rise in a warm place for 1 hour, or until doubled in size. Bake at 375 degrees for 35 to 40 minutes, or until brown. (If the brioche darkens too much during baking, cover with a piece of aluminum foil.) Remove the brioche from the pan and cool on a wire rack. When cool, trim the ends from the brioche and cut into 4½-inch slices. Trim each slice into a 2½-inch square, place on a sheet pan, and toast in the oven at 325 degrees for 5 minutes on each side, or until golden brown.

To make the tuiles: Use an offset spatula to spread about 1 to 1½ teaspoons of the Vanilla Tuile Batter into a 3- to 3½-inch circle on a Silpat-lined or nonstick sheet pan. Repeat until there are at least 6 tuiles, to allow for breakage. Bake at 325 degrees for 5 to 7 minutes, or until light golden brown. Remove the tuiles from the oven and immediately form them into small cup shapes by draping them over small inverted ramekins or cups. If the tuiles harden before they are removed from the sheet pan, they can be returned to the oven to soften.

ASSEMBLY Place a brioche square in the center of each plate. Top with the Ugli fruit segments on one half and the pink grapefruit segments on the other half, reserving the liquid. Spoon 2 tablespoons of the Crème Fraîche Sabayon down the center of the fruit and brown with a blowtorch for 5 to 10 seconds, or until the sabayon starts to brown. Place a tuile cup on one corner of the fruit and place a small scoop of Pink Grapefruit–Chile-Tequila Sorbet in the cup. Drizzle 1 tablespoon of the honey-juice mixture around each plate.

Crème Fraîche Sabayon

Yield: ½ to ¾ cup

3 egg yolks

1/3 cup Vanilla Simple Syrup (see Appendices)

3 tablespoons crème fraîche

METHOD Prepare an ice water bath. Whisk the egg yolks and Vanilla Simple Syrup in a metal bowl over barely simmering water for 10 to 15 minutes, or until it is at least double in volume and reaches the ribbon stage. Cool over the ice water bath, stirring occasionally, until chilled, and fold in the crème fraîche.

Pink Grapefruit–Chile-Tequila Sorbet

Yield: 1 quart

2 large pears, peeled, cored, and chopped

3/4 cup Simple Syrup (see Appendices)

1 jalepeño, stemmed, halved, and seeded

2 pink grapefruits, skin and pith removed, quartered, and any juice reserved

1 cup freshly squeezed orange juice

1/4 cup corn syrup

1/4 cup tequila

METHOD Put the pears, Simple Syrup, and jalepeño in a medium saucepan and add water, if necessary, to cover the pears. Bring to a simmer and cook for 15 to 20 minutes, or until the pears are tender. Remove the pears, and reduce the remaining liquid to ¾ cup. Place the pears, grapefruit (and any juice), orange juice, and reduced cooking liquid in a blender. Purée by pulsing, taking care not to run the blender continuously and overblend. Add the corn syrup and tequila and let the mixture cool. Freeze in an ice cream machine and keep frozen until ready to use.

Buddha's Hand Fruit Confit
with Mango Sorbet

Although it is unusual, the citrus fruit known as Buddha's hand fruit
is becoming more readily available and can be ordered from many produce markets.
It is too bitter to eat raw, but after being poached several times in water
and candied in Simple Syrup, the subtle, citrus flavor of the fruit reveals itself.
The poached fruit has a texture that is barely resistant to the bite and
provides a pleasant mouthfeel. A scoop of mango or peppered pineapple sorbet
is the perfect finale to this light, tropical dessert.

Serves 4

2 small Buddha's hand fruit
1 cup Simple Syrup (see Appendices)
2¼ cups water
1 cup freshly squeezed lemon juice
½ cup sugar
Mango Sorbet (recipe follows)

METHOD To prepare the fruit: Cut off and reserve the fingers of the Buddha's hand. Using a mandolin, thinly slice the remaining fruit. Blanch the slices in boiling water, drain, and repeat the process once. Bring ½ cup of the Simple Syrup, 1 cup of the water, and ½ cup of the lemon juice to a boil. Add the blanched slices, simmer for 5 minutes, and set aside in the syrup.

Blanch the Buddha's hand fingers in boiling water seven times, draining after each blanching. Bring 1 cup of the water and the remaining ½ cup of the lemon juice and ½ cup Simple Syrup to a boil. Add the blanched fingers, simmer for 10 minutes, and set aside in the syrup.

Just before serving, cook the sugar and the remaining ¼ cup water in a heavy-bottomed sauté pan over medium heat for about 5 minutes, or until the caramel is just turning golden. Add the Buddha's hand fingers, toss them in the caramel, and keep warm.

ASSEMBLY Spoon some of the sliced fruit in the center of each plate. Top with a quenelle of Mango Sorbet and arrange the Buddha hand fingers around the sorbet. Drizzle some of the caramel around the plate.

Mango Sorbet

Yield: approximately 1 quart

3 ripe mangoes, peeled and chopped
(about 3 cups)
¼ cup freshly squeezed lime juice
½ cup water
⅓ cup Simple Syrup (see Appendices)

METHOD Combine all of the ingredients in a blender and purée for 3 minutes, or until smooth. Strain through a fine-mesh sieve, refrigerate to chill, and then freeze in an ice cream machine. Keep frozen until ready to use.

Satsuma Orange–Chocolate Custard with Candied Meyer Lemon and Hazelnut Tuiles

I love the combination of orange and chocolate; the two flavors blend together perfectly.
The orange provides enough delicately playful citrus to cut the richness of the chocolate
without being so tart that it diminishes the chocolate's splendor. In this preparation,
a disc of creamy chocolate-orange custard is sandwiched between two crispy hazelnut tuiles.
The sandwich is placed on some slices of sweet-tart Meyer lemon confit.
In all, the package of flavors and textures is quite heady, but still fairly light.

Serves 6

2 tablespoons sugar

6 egg yolks

2¼ cups heavy cream

4 satsuma oranges, zested, segments reserved and zest chopped

4½ ounces bittersweet chocolate, chopped

½ cup Simple Syrup (see Appendices)

Candied Meyer Lemon (recipe follows)

Hazelnut Tuiles (recipe follows)

Chocolate-Satsuma Orange Sauce (recipe follows)

METHOD To make the custard: Whisk the sugar and egg yolks in a double boiler over barely simmering water for 10 minutes, or until tripled in volume. Bring the cream and orange zest to a boil and pour over the chocolate, stirring until the chocolate is completely melted. Pour the chocolate over the egg mixture, and cook over barely simmering water for 25 minutes, or until the mixture has thickened to a pudding consistency. Strain through a fine-mesh sieve. Lightly oil the outsides of six 2½-inch-diameter by 1½-inch-high ring molds and wrap the bottoms in plastic wrap. Spoon the custard into the molds and refrigerate.

To prepare the orange segments: Cook the orange segments in the Simple Syrup for 5 minutes, or until just warm.

ASSEMBLY Arrange a few warm orange segments in the center of each plate, reserving the cooking liquid. Lay some of the Candied Meyer Lemon slices around the oranges. Unmold the 6 custards onto 6 of the Hazelnut Tuiles, remove the ring molds, and top each custard with another tuile. Place a custard sandwich on top of the oranges and drizzle the cooking liquid from the oranges and the Chocolate-Satsuma Orange Sauce around the plates.

Candied Meyer Lemon

Yield: approximately 1 cup

3 Meyer lemons, thinly sliced, with peel
½ cup sugar
1 cup water

METHOD Blanch the lemon slices in boiling water and strain. Repeat this process two more times. Bring the sugar and water to a boil in a medium saucepan. Add the lemon slices and simmer gently for 20 to 30 minutes, or until the liquid is syrupy and the lemons are candied. Cool in the syrup.

Hazelnut Tuiles

Yield: approximately 1 cup of batter

2 tablespoons unsalted butter
¼ cup confectioners' sugar
3 tablespoons honey
⅓ cup flour
⅓ cup ground toasted hazelnuts

METHOD Cream the butter and sugar. Add the honey, flour, and nuts and mix well. Using a rolling pin, roll the mixture between 2 sheets of parchment paper until paper-thin. Place the dough on a sheet pan and put it in the freezer to harden. Remove the top sheet of parchment, place the dough on a Silpat-lined or nonstick sheet pan with the parchment on top, remove the parchment, and bake at 350 degrees for 10 minutes, or until golden brown. Remove from the oven and immediately cut into 2½-inch circles using a lightly oiled ring cutter. Remove the cut out tuiles from the pan and cool on a counter or another flat surface.

Chocolate–Satsuma Orange Sauce

Yield: approximately ½ cup

½ cup freshly squeezed satsuma orange juice
1 tablespoon sugar
2 ounces bittersweet chocolate, chopped

METHOD Heat the orange juice and sugar over medium-low heat until just warm and the sugar is dissolved. Whisk the juice into the chocolate to melt the chocolate. Warm before serving.

Berries

Berry flavors vary from the slight tartness of raspberries to the richness of black raspberries or blueberries, and the wine pairings for them will be equally diverse.  The wines can range from an aromatic Gewürztraminer, such as a Selection des Grains Nobles from Alsace, which is ideal for more tart and aromatic berries, to the sweet, concentrated fruit of a Black Muscat for partnering with richer berries. Sweet Red Wine, by Ca' Togni Vineyards, is a unique wine made from Black Hamburg or Muscat grapes and the perfect complement to almost any berry dessert. Quady Vineyards uses the same grapes to produce wines that range from a sweet effervescent style all the way to a rich fruity style. There is also a broad range of lightly fortified wines, made from various berries and fruits, which echo the flavors of the fruits in these desserts. Winemaker Randall Grahm makes a Creme de Cassis—style wine, Bonny Doon Framboise, which has enough fruit and acidity to make it a great accompaniment to any sweet berry dessert.

Strawberry-Almond Shortcake with Basil

*Everyone loves the classic strawberry shortcake, but sometimes a more refined presentation
is welcome. This dish is easy to prepare and truly emphasizes the glorious flavor of the strawberries,
or any berry, in the height of their season. The components of this dish can be prepared well in
advance and assembled at the last moment. This dessert stands alone nicely as the sole finishing point
of a meal, or it makes a wonderful introduction to something more substantial like chocolate.
The serving size is easily adjusted to suit any occasion. For a variation, try substituting
chopped candied ginger or ground praline for the vanilla in the crème fraîche.*

Serves 6

1 cup unsalted butter

1/2 cup plus 2 tablespoons sugar

1 cup whole toasted almonds, skin on

2 cups flour

Pinch of salt

*2 tablespoons sliced almonds, skin on,
lightly toasted*

2 cups strawberries, cut into wedges

1/4 cup Simple Syrup (see Appendices)

1 teaspoon lime zest

1/2 cup crème fraîche

1 cup heavy cream

Pulp of 1/2 vanilla bean

2 tablespoons aged balsamic vinegar

Basil Syrup (recipe follows)

2 tablespoons tiny fresh basil leaves

METHOD To make the shortcake: Cream the butter and 6 tablespoons of the sugar until light, fluffy, and almost white. Purée the whole almonds for 2 minutes, or until very fine, and add to the butter mixture along with the flour and salt. Mix until just combined. Roll out the dough between 2 sheets of plastic wrap until 1/8 inch thick. Lay the sheet of shortcake dough on a sheet pan, still covered in the plastic wrap, and refrigerate for 30 minutes. Remove the plastic wrap, place the dough on a cutting board, and cut into at least thirty 1 1/2 by 2-inch rectangles. Place on a parchment-lined sheet pan and lightly press 2 or 3 almond slices into each rectangle. Bake at 350 degrees for 15 to 20 minutes, or until golden brown.

To prepare the strawberries: Toss the strawberry wedges with the Simple Syrup and lime zest.

To make the cream: Whisk the crème fraîche, heavy cream, the remaining 1/4 cup of sugar, and the vanilla pulp until soft peaks form.

ASSEMBLY Spoon some of the strawberry wedges in the center of each plate and drizzle with the balsamic vinegar and the Basil Syrup. Layer the almond squares with the cream mixture until there are 6 separate stacks of 5 almond squares. Set the stacks sideways on top of the strawberries and sprinkle with the basil leaves.

Basil Syrup

Yield: 1/2 cup

1/2 cup fresh basil leaves

1/4 cup fresh spinach leaves

1/4 cup Simple Syrup (see Appendices)

METHOD Blanch the basil and spinach in boiling water for 10 seconds. Remove from the pan and immediately shock in ice water. Squeeze any excess water from the leaves and coarsely chop. Purée with the Simple Syrup for 3 minutes, or until bright green. Strain through a fine-mesh sieve. Store in the refrigerator until ready to use.

Huckleberry Tuiles with
White and Golden Peach Compote
and Huckleberry Sherbet

*Huckleberries and peaches are a great combination. The refined acid of the berries
cuts the sweetness of the peaches, creating a perfect marriage of flavors.
The huckleberries in this dish appear in three different ways, providing a variety of textures:
chewy fruit tuiles, icy sherbet, and smooth whole berries. This dish would be a big hit at a spa,
as it's packed with flavor and is almost fat free. This could also be made
with blueberries, blackberries, or raspberries with good results.*

Serves 4

2 white peaches
1 golden peach
1/4 cup water
1/2 cup freshly squeezed lemon juice
2 tablespoons sugar
1/2 cup Simple Syrup (see Appendices)
1 cup huckleberries, hulls removed
Huckleberry Tuiles (recipe follows)
Huckleberry Sherbet (recipe follows)

METHOD To prepare the peaches: Blanch the peaches in boiling water for 1 minute, immediately shock in ice water, and peel, reserving the skins. Cut the golden peach and 1 of the white peaches into small dice and set the diced fruit aside in separate bowls. Bring the skins, water, 1/4 cup of the lemon juice, and the sugar to a boil, then simmer for 10 minutes. Pour the mixture into a blender and purée for 2 minutes, or until smooth, and strain through a fine-mesh sieve. Divide the liquid between the bowls of diced peaches.

To make the peach sauce: Chop the remaining white peach and purée in a blender with 1/4 cup of the Simple Syrup and the remaining 1/4 cup of lemon juice for 2 minutes, or until smooth. Strain through a fine-mesh sieve.

To prepare the huckleberries: Heat the huckleberries with the remaining 1/4 cup of Simple Syrup until warm.

ASSEMBLY Place 4 Huckleberry Tuile rings in the center of each plate. Spoon the diced yellow peach into the first and third tuiles. Spoon the diced white peach into the second and fourth tuiles. Spoon some of the warm huckleberries over the peaches and around the plates. Drizzle the huckleberry cooking juice and peach sauce around the plates. Place a quenelle of Huckleberry Sherbet in the center of the tuiles.

Huckleberry Tuiles

Yield: approximately 1 1/2 cups batter

1/2 cup huckleberries
1/4 cup mashed banana
1/4 cup water
1 egg white
1 1/2 tablespoons sugar

METHOD Bring the huckleberries, banana, and water to a boil. Purée the mixture in a blender with the egg white for 2 minutes, or until smooth. Make a 1 by 4 1/2-inch template from heavy plastic or cardboard. Spread a thin layer of the batter inside the template on a Silpat-lined or nonstick sheet pan and sprinkle with the sugar. Repeat until there are at least 16 tuiles (the extras allow for breakage). Bake at 225 degrees for 40 minutes, or until set. Immediately remove the tuiles from the sheet pan and mold each one around a dowel or other 1- to 1 1/4-inch diameter circular mold and set aside. If the tuiles harden on the sheet pan, they can be returned to the oven to soften.

Huckleberry Sherbet

Yield: about 1 pint
1 1/2 cups huckleberries
1/2 cup milk
6 tablespoons sugar

METHOD Combine all of the ingredients in a blender and purée for 3 minutes, or until smooth. Strain through a fine-mesh sieve and freeze in an ice cream machine. Keep frozen until ready to use.

Fraises des Bois Linzertorte
with Primrose Emulsion

As a young cook, one of the first things I learned to make was a classic linzertorte.
I enjoyed the raspberry filling, but what I really loved was the buttery, hazelnut-flavored
linzer dough. It literally melts in your mouth, and using fraises des bois instead of the traditional
raspberries elevates this dessert to the realm of the sublime. Almonds or pine nuts can be substituted
in the dough for interesting variation, but the hazelnuts are the most magical with the berries.
If wild strawberries are not available, you can substitute figs, or even apricots, with great results.
For a richer dessert, place a scoop of vanilla ice cream on top of the tortes.
The individual linzertortes are a great way to impress your guests,
but you could also make this in one 8-inch tart pan to save some time.

Serves 6

¾ cup unsalted butter

1 cup confectioners' sugar

1½ teaspoons lemon zest

1 tablespoon orange zest

3 egg yolks

1⅔ cups flour

1 teaspoon baking powder

2 teaspoons ground cinnamon

1 teaspoon ground nutmeg

¼ teaspoon salt

1½ cups toasted, ground hazelnuts

2 cups red fraises des bois, stems removed

1 tablespoon cornstarch

2 tablespoons granulated sugar

1 egg, whisked

White and Red Fraises des Bois Sauces
(recipe follows)

Primrose Emulsion (recipe follows)

½ cup red fraises des bois, with stems

½ cup white fraises des bois, with stems

4 primroses, petals julienned

METHOD To make the tart shells: Cream the butter, confectioners' sugar, and lemon and orange zests until well mixed. Add the egg yolks and mix until just combined. Add the flour, baking powder, cinnamon, nutmeg, salt, and hazelnuts and continue mixing until just combined. Refrigerate the dough for several hours and then roll out between 2 sheets of parchment to about ⅛ inch thick. Cut six 4-inch circles and press the circles into 3-inch-diameter by ½-inch-high tart rings. Cut the remaining dough into thirty-six ¼-inch-wide strips to use for the lattice (a crimped cutter works well). Place the dough strips and tart rings on a sheet pan, cover with plastic wrap, and refrigerate for 1 hour.

To make the tarts: Toss together the stemmed red fraises des bois, cornstarch, and granulated sugar. Distribute the mixture evenly among the tart rings. Weave the dough strips into a lattice on top of each tart, trim the excess dough, and brush with the whisked egg. Refrigerate for 2 hours and bake at 350 degrees for 25 minutes, or until golden brown. Let cool slightly and then loosen the tarts from the sides of the tart rings with a small paring knife and remove the tart rings.

ASSEMBLY Place a tart in the center of each plate. Drizzle the white Fraises des Bois Sauce, red Fraises des Bois Sauce, and the froth from the Primrose Emulsion around the tarts. Arrange some of the red and white fraises des bois around the plate and sprinkle with the julienned primrose petals.

White and Red Fraises des Bois Sauces

Yield: approximately ¾ cup each

1 cup red fraises des bois

½ cup sugar

¼ cup freshly squeezed lemon juice

1 cup white fraises des bois

METHOD Cook the red fraises des bois, ¼ cup of the sugar, and 2 tablespoons of the lemon juice until it just starts to boil. Remove from the heat and purée for 2 minutes, or until smooth. Strain through a fine-mesh sieve and set aside. Repeat the process with the white fraises des bois, but do not strain after puréeing.

Primrose Emulsion

Yield: approximately 1 cup

⅓ cup freshly squeezed orange juice

6 primroses, petals removed

½ cup crème fraîche

¼ cup Simple Syrup (see Appendices)

METHOD Purée the orange juice and primrose petals for 1 minute and strain through a fine-mesh sieve. Warm the juice mixture, crème fraîche, and Simple Syrup. Blend with a handheld blender, until frothy, just before serving.

Napoleon of White Fraises des Bois
and Golden Raspberries with
Pink Peppercorn Meringues and Thyme

*This dish can be prepared with any type of berry, or even other fruits, but using fraises des bois
or golden raspberries makes it a special treat. The delicate pink peppercorn meringues
leave a delightful, barely sharp flavor that is not so strong as to overpower the berries.
Petals of thyme add another enticing flavor element. In all, this preparation is simple, but striking.*

Serves 6

3 egg whites

1/2 cup plus 2 tablespoons granulated sugar

2 tablespoons pink peppercorns

1 1/4 cups milk

2 tablespoons heavy cream

2 teaspoons chopped fresh thyme

4 egg yolks

1 1/2 tablespoons cornstarch

1 tablespoon unsalted butter

2 tablespoons crème fraîche

2 to 3 thyme sprigs

1 tablespoon confectioners' sugar

2 cups fresh golden raspberries

2 cups white fraises des bois

METHOD To make the meringue: Whisk the egg whites until they form soft peaks. Add 6 tablespoons of the granulated sugar and whisk until stiff. Spread the egg whites about 1/8 inch thick onto a Silpat-lined or nonstick half sheet pan. Crush the pink peppercorns and rub two-thirds of them through a sieve over the meringue. Bake at 225 degrees for 1 to 1 1/2 hours, or until lightly colored and dry. Remove the pan from the oven. Place the meringue on a cutting board while still warm and use a long, serrated knife to cut the meringues into 1 by 3-inch rectangles.

To make the cream: Prepare an ice water bath. Bring the milk, cream, and chopped thyme to a boil in a saucepan. Whisk together the egg yolks, the remaining 4 tablespoons of granulated sugar, and the cornstarch in a small bowl. Slowly pour in some of the hot cream mixture to temper the eggs. Pour the egg mixture into the cream and bring to a boil, whisking continuously. Strain through a fine-mesh sieve and whisk in the butter. Cool over the ice water bath, stirring occasionally, until chilled. Fold in the crème fraîche just prior to serving.

To prepare the thyme garnish: Toss the thyme sprigs with the confectioners' sugar until coated and shake in a sieve to remove the excess sugar.

ASSEMBLY Place 1 meringue rectangle in the center of each plate. Top with a spoonful of the cream mixture and some of the golden raspberries. Place a meringue rectangle on the berries and spoon on some of the cream mixture. Arrange the white fraises des bois on the cream and top with another meringue rectangle. Spoon some of the cream on top of the meringue and sprinkle the thyme sprigs over the top and around the base of the dessert. Rub the remaining pink peppercorns through a sieve over the top of the cream and around the plate

Warm Fig Turnovers with Strawberries and Strawberry-Chartreuse Ice Cream

This is a dish in which ordinary ingredients are combined for an extraordinary result. The warm figs oozing from the center of these turnovers burst with flavor and succulence. The strawberries provide just the right sweet-acidic contrast to the lush figs and flaky pastry, and the exotic Strawberry-Chartreuse Ice Cream adds creaminess and comforting richness. As a final, piercing textural and flavor note, Oven-Dried Strawberry Chips are chopped and used to coat the ice cream. Apricots or peaches could also be used in place of the figs for an interesting flavor variation.

Serves 4

1/2 cup granulated sugar

1/4 cup water

2 tablespoons freshly squeezed lemon juice

1/4 cup crème fraîche

4 fresh figs, quartered lengthwise

Cream Cheese Dough (see Appendices)

1 egg, beaten

Confectioners' sugar, for dusting

1 cup sliced strawberries, some with stems

1/4 cup Chartreuse liqueur

*Strawberry-Chartreuse Ice Cream
(recipe follows)*

Oven-Dried Strawberry Chips, coarsely chopped (see Appendices)

METHOD To make the filling: Cook the granulated sugar and water in a small, heavy-bottomed sauté pan over medium heat for 5 minutes, or until golden brown. Add the lemon juice and crème fraîche and stir. Add the figs, remove from heat, and cool. Use a slotted spoon to remove the figs, reserving the fig-caramel sauce. Rewarm the sauce just prior to serving, adding a little water, if necessary.

To make the turnovers: Roll out the Cream Cheese Dough to 1/8 inch thick. Using a ravioli cutter, cut eight 2-inch squares. Place 2 fig quarters on each square, trimming the figs if they are too large. Fold the dough over the top of the figs to form a triangle shape, brush the pointed tip with some of the egg, and pinch the tip to seal. Brush the top of the turnovers with the egg and bake at 350 degrees for 30 minutes, or until golden brown. Set aside to cool. Sprinkle the cooled turnovers with confectioners' sugar before serving.

To prepare the strawberries: Combine the strawberries and Chartreuse in a small bowl and marinate for 3 minutes.

ASSEMBLY Spoon some of the strawberries and the liquid onto the center of each plate. Place 2 turnovers on the strawberries. Roll 4 small scoops of the Strawberry-Chartreuse Ice Cream in the Oven-Dried Strawberry Chips and place one on top of each set of turnovers. Drizzle the fig-caramel sauce around the plate and sprinkle with more chopped Oven-Dried Strawberry Chips.

Strawberry-Chartreuse Ice Cream

Yield: approximately 3 cups

1/2 cup Chartreuse liqueur

2 cups heavy cream

1/2 cup strawberries, hulled and coarsely chopped

4 egg yolks

1/4 cup sugar

METHOD Prepare an ice water bath. Simmer the Chartreuse until reduced by half. In a separate pan, bring the cream and strawberries to a boil. Whisk together the egg yolks and sugar and slowly pour in some of the hot cream mixture to temper the eggs. Pour the egg mixture into the cream and cook for 2 to 3 minutes, or until the mixture coats the back of a spoon and steam rises from the top. Strain through a fine-mesh sieve, pressing on the berries. Add the reduced Chartreuse and cool over the ice water bath until chilled. Freeze in an ice cream machine and keep frozen until ready to use.

Poppyseed Angel Food Cake
with Stewed Blueberries and
Red Wine–Black Pepper Penna Gelato

This delicate, spongy angel food cake is the perfect contrast to the luscious berry compote because
of the greatly contrasting textures. The penna gelato is richer than a sorbet but not as cloying
as ice cream and has the lush, concentrated fruitiness of red wine to further amplify the berry flavor.
The black pepper is the perfect finish; it cuts all of the flavors and creates a pop of unexpected heat.

Serves 6

5 tablespoons cake flour

³/₄ cup plus 2 tablespoons sugar

¹/₂ cup egg whites (4 to 5 egg whites)

¹/₂ teaspoon cream of tartar

Pinch of salt

1 tablespoon poppyseeds

1¹/₂ teaspoons lemon zest, finely chopped

2 tablespoons water

2 cups blueberries

Red Wine–Black Pepper Penna Gelato
(recipe follows)

2 tablespoons crème fraîche

METHOD To make the cake: Sift the cake flour and 2 tablespoons of the sugar together, and set aside. Whip the egg whites and cream of tartar until soft peaks form. Slowly add the salt and ¹/₄ cup of the sugar and continue to whip until stiff peaks form. Fold the flour mixture into the egg whites.

Fold the poppyseeds and lemon zest into the mixture. Place six 2¹/₂-inch ring molds on a parchment-lined sheet pan. Fill the mold three-quarters of the way full with the poppyseed batter and bake at 375 degrees for 12 minutes, or until slightly golden brown. Cool briefly, and remove from the molds.

To make the compote: Place the remaining ¹/₂ cup sugar and the water in a medium sauté pan and cook over medium heat for 10 to 12 minutes, or until the sugar is golden brown and caramelized. Add the blueberries and continue to cook for 3 minutes to dissolve any hardened sugar and heat the berries.

ASSEMBLY Spoon some of the blueberry compote in the center of each plate and top with an angel food cake. Place a scoop of Red Wine–Black Pepper Penna Gelato on top of each cake and drizzle the crème fraîche over the blueberries.

Red Wine–Black Pepper Penna Gelato

Yield: about 3 cups

3 cups red wine

1 tablespoon black pepper

1 cup heavy cream

3 cups milk

6 tablespoons sugar

2 tablespoons corn syrup

METHOD Prepare an ice water bath. Simmer the red wine for 20 to 25 minutes, or until reduced to ¹/₂ cup. Add the pepper, cover, and steep for 30 minutes. In a separate saucepan, simmer the cream and milk for 30 minutes, or until reduced to 2 cups. Whisk in the sugar and corn syrup and cook for 3 minutes, or until all of the sugar is dissolved. Whisk in the red wine. Strain through a fine-mesh sieve, cool in the ice water bath, and freeze in an ice cream machine. Keep frozen until ready to use.

Tropical Fruits

Tropical fruits have exotic aromas, rich textures, and very sweet flavors that require wines even sweeter and richer than the fruits themselves. Fortified styles of liqueur Muscat and liqueur Tokay from Australia are wonderful accompaniments to the sticky sweetness of these tropical fruits. Merryvale Vineyards in California produces the equally good, extended wood-aged Muscat de Frontignan. These liqueur-style Muscats almost taste like a Tawny Port yet the aromatic fruit characteristics of the Muscat are still present and interplay wonderfully with the fruits. An unfortified style of Muskat Ottonel from Burgenland, Austria, also works well. Try the Muskat Ottonel Beerenauslese from Alois Kracher. It is intensely sweet with beautiful orange and tropical fruit aromas that are perfect with delicate desserts.

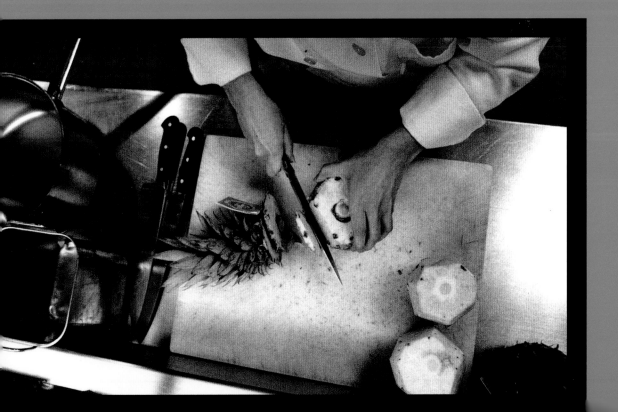

Pineapple Tarte Tatin with Ginger–Hokkaido Squash Ice Cream

*The caramelized fruit in a tarte tatin is a truly delectable taste and texture sensation—
glazed, sweet, and oozing with flavor. In this dish pineapple is substituted for the traditional apple or
pear with stunning results. The satiny Ginger–Hokkaido Squash Ice Cream provides an exotic but
earthy flavor that magnificently complements the slightly astringent but caramely, sweet pineapple.
This dessert is just as wonderful hot out of the oven as it is at room temperature.*

Serves 6

Cream Cheese Dough (see Appendices)
1 pineapple, peeled
1 cup sugar
¼ cup water
*Ginger–Hokkaido Squash Ice Cream
(recipe follows)*

METHOD To prepare the crust: Roll out the Cream Cheese Dough to ¼ inch thick. Cut into six 2½-inch circles, cover, and refrigerate until ready to use.

To prepare the pineapple: Cut the pineapple into 3 pieces by making a vertical cut on each side of the core. Discard the core. Cut the remaining pineapple into twelve ¼-inch-thick slices. Lay out 2 slices of pineapple, flat sides together, and trim to form a 2½-inch circle. Repeat with the remaining pineapple slices.

To make the caramel: Cook the sugar and water in a large, heavy-bottomed sauté pan over medium heat for 10 minutes, or until golden brown and caramelized.

To assemble the tart: Wrap the bottoms of six 2½-inch-diameter by 1½-inch-high ring molds in aluminum foil and place them on a sheet pan. Spoon some of the caramel into each ring mold and swirl to coat the bottom. Top with a circle of pineapple and then a circle of Cream Cheese Dough. Bake at 350 degrees for 30 to 40 minutes, or until golden brown.

ASSEMBLY Remove the tartes from the oven and immediately invert onto serving plates. Place a quenelle of Ginger–Hokkaido Squash Ice Cream next to each tart.

Ginger–Hokkaido Squash Ice Cream

Yield: approximately 3 cups

2 cups heavy cream
2 tablespoons peeled and chopped fresh ginger
4 egg yolks
¼ cup sugar
½ cup cooked hokkaido squash, puréed
Dash of lemon juice

METHOD Prepare an ice water bath. Bring the cream and ginger to a boil. Cover, remove from the heat, and steep for 30 minutes. Return the cream to a boil. Whisk together the egg yolks and sugar and pour in some of the hot cream mixture to temper the eggs. Pour the eggs into the cream mixture and continue cooking for 3 to 4 minutes, or until the mixture coats the back of a spoon and steam rises from the top. Cool in the ice water bath, stirring occasionally, until chilled. Mix in the squash, add the lemon juice to taste, and strain through a fine-mesh sieve. Freeze in an ice cream machine and keep frozen until ready to use.

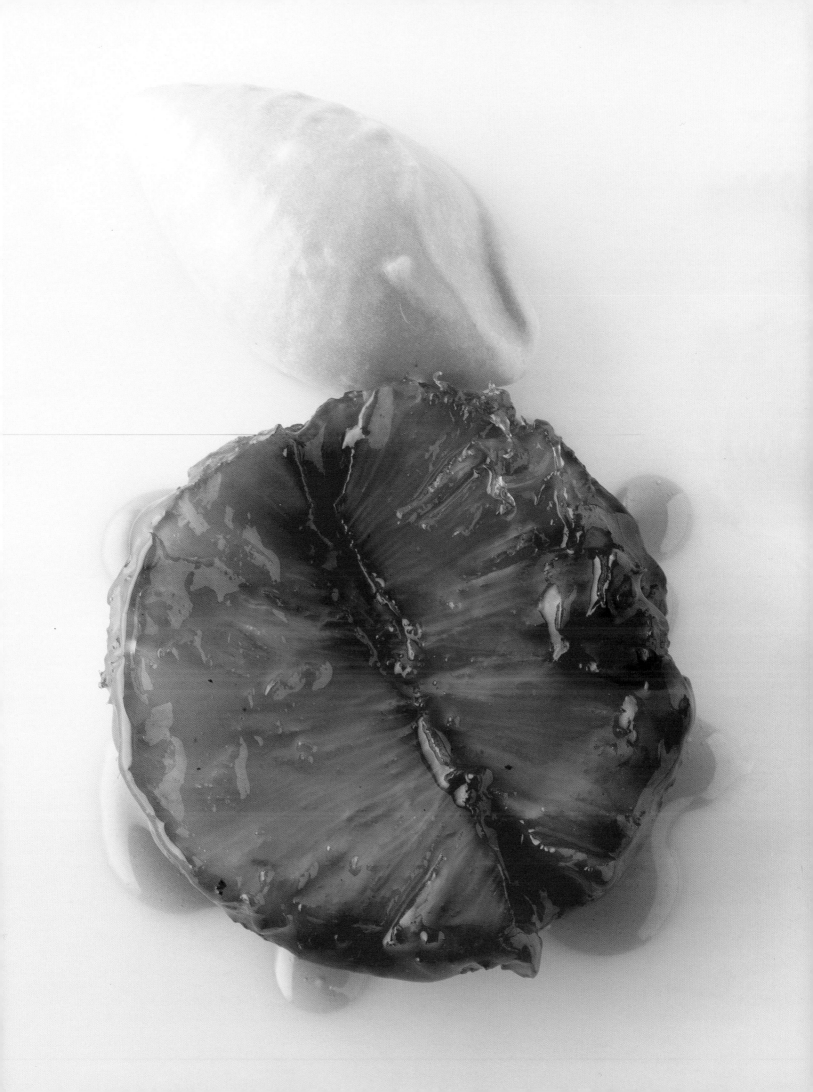

Tropical Fruit Ice Cream Terrine with Their Fruit Compotes and Hickory Nut Praline

~~~~~~

This ice cream terrine is fairly easy to make. All you need is a terrine mold and tempered ice cream.
I make my own ice creams, but a high-quality store-bought variety would also work.
The intention is merely to present a serving of ice cream in a playful and visually appealing manner.
In this dish the terrine sits on a piece of crispy filo that not only supports the terrine
but provides a nice textural counterbalance to the smooth ice cream and unctuous fruits.
The refined richness of the hickory nut sauce pushes this dessert over the top.

Serves 6

8 cups heavy cream

2 teaspoons lime zest

16 egg yolks

2 cups granulated sugar

³/₄ cup chico sapote purée

6 tablespoons freshly squeezed lime juice

³/₄ cup mango purée

2 tablespoons orange zest

¹/₂ cup mamey sapote purée

1 cup freshly squeezed orange juice

³/₄ cup Barbados cherry purée

¹/₂ cup peeled and chopped chico sapote

¹/₂ cup peeled and chopped mango

¹/₂ cup peeled and chopped mamey sapote

¹/₂ cup peeled and chopped Barbados cherries

³/₄ cup Simple Syrup (see Appendices)

¹/₂ cup Hickory Nut Praline, finely chopped (see Appendices)

¹/₂ cup toasted hickory nuts

4 to 6 tablespoons milk

Filo bases (see Appendices)

METHOD To make the chico sapote and mango ice creams: Prepare an ice water bath. Bring 4 cups of the cream and the lime zest to a boil. Whisk together 8 of the egg yolks and 1 cup of the granulated sugar and pour in some of the hot cream to temper the eggs. Pour the eggs into the cream and cook for 2 to 3 minutes, or until the mixture coats the back of a spoon and steam rises from the top. Strain through a fine-mesh sieve and cool over an ice water bath, stirring occasionally, until chilled.

In a small bowl, mix the chico sapote purée with 3 tablespoons of the lime juice. Add this mixture to half of the cream mixture and freeze in an ice cream machine. Spread the ice cream in a 1-inch-thick layer in an 8 by 8-inch pan, cover with plastic wrap, and freeze until firm.

In another small bowl, mix the mango purée with the remaining 3 tablespoons of lime juice. Add this mixture to the remaining cream mixture and freeze in an ice cream machine. Spread the ice cream in a 1-inch-thick layer in an 8 by 8-inch pan, cover with plastic wrap, and freeze until firm.

To make the mamey sapote–lime and Barbados cherry ice creams: Bring the remaining 4 cups of cream and the orange zest to a boil. Whisk together the remaining 8 egg yolks and 1 cup of granulated sugar and pour in some of the hot cream to temper the eggs. Pour the eggs into the cream and cook for 2 or 3 minutes, or until the mixture coats the back of a spoon and steam rises from the top. Strain through a fine-mesh sieve and cool over the ice water bath, stirring occasionally, until chilled.

In another small bowl, mix the mamey sapote with ½ cup of the orange juice. Add to half of the cream mixture and freeze in an ice cream machine. Spread the ice cream in a 1-inch-thick layer in an 8 by 8-inch pan, cover with plastic wrap, and freeze until firm.

Combine the Barbados cherry purée with the remaining ½ cup of orange juice. Add to the remaining cream mixture and freeze in an ice cream machine. Spread in a 1-inch-thick layer in an 8 by 8-inch pan, cover with plastic wrap, and freeze until firm.

To make the terrine: Remove the plastic wrap and turn the ice cream out onto a cutting board. Trim the edge and cut a ³/₄ by 8-inch strip from each ice cream, returning each pan to the freezer after the ice cream is cut. Place the strip of mango ice cream and mamey sapote–lime ice cream in the bottom of a 1³/₄ by 2¹/₄ by 8-inch plastic wrap–lined terrine mold and press firmly. Place the strip of Barbados cherry ice cream on top of the mango ice cream and the chico sapote ice cream on top of the mamey sapote ice cream and press firmly. Freeze for at least 30 minutes before slicing.

To make the compotes: Warm the chopped chico sapote, mango, mamey sapote, and Barbados cherry separately in 3 tablespoons of Simple Syrup each.

To make the sauce: Purée 2 tablespoons of the Hickory Nut Praline, the hickory nuts, and milk for 3 minutes, or until smooth. Add additional milk to thin to a sauce consistency, if necessary.

ASSEMBLY Lay 1 of the filo circles in the center of each plate. Spoon some of each of the warm fruit compotes around the filo and top the filo circle with a filo rectangle. Cut the ice cream terrine into ³/₄-inch-thick slices with a hot knife and place a slice on each of the filo rectangles. Drizzle the hickory nut sauce around the plate and sprinkle with the remaining Hickory Nut Praline.

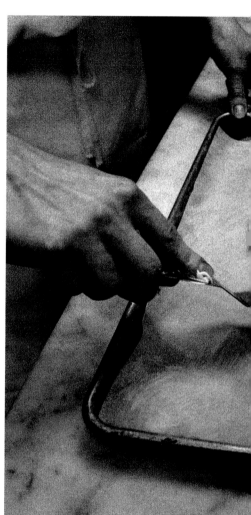

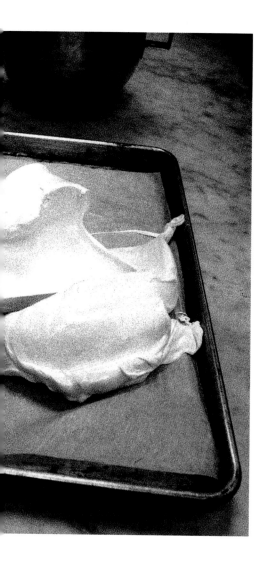
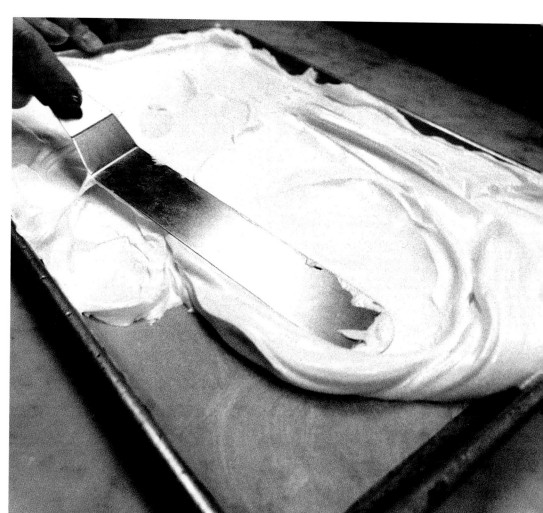

Mamey Sapote Beggar's Purse with Tropical Fruits and Mamey Sapote Ice Cream

*Fully ripe mamey sapote has a lush, creamy, tropical sweet potato flavor,
without the starchy quality of potatoes. Sweet potatoes can be substituted for the mamey
in the beggar's purses if mamey is unavailable. The crunchy filo, creamy mamey and mango,
and the firmer, more acidic pineapple combine to create a great balance of flavors and textures.
This dessert can be served hot out of the oven or at room temperature. I like to serve it hot so I can
enjoy the temperature contrast of the ice cream melting into the hot pastry and succulent fruit.*

Serves 6

1 small mamey sapote, peeled and diced (about 1 cup)

1 cup granulated sugar

1/4 cup diced fresh pineapple

1/2 cup peeled and diced mango

2 tablespoons crème fraîche

1 1/2 teaspoons chopped lemon zest

6 sheets filo dough

6 tablespoons unsalted butter, melted

Confectioners' sugar, for dusting

1/4 cup water

3 apples, peeled and diced

Caramel–Kaffir Lime Sauce (recipe follows)

1 tablespoon julienned kaffir lime leaves

Mamey Sapote Ice Cream (recipe follows)

METHOD To make the filling: Combine the mamey sapote, 1/2 cup of the granulated sugar, the pineapple, mango, crème fraîche, and lemon zest in a small bowl.

To assemble the beggar's purses: Lay out a sheet of filo on the work surface, brush with 1 tablespoon of the melted butter, sprinkle with the confectioners' sugar, and top with another sheet of filo. Brush the filo with 1 tablespoon of the butter, sprinkle with confect   top with another sheet of filo, and   with 1 tablespoon of the butter. Repeat this process with the 3 remaining sheets of filo. Cut both stacks of sheets into three 6-inch squares. Using a slotted spoon, place some of the fruit filling in the center of each square. Shape the filo into beggar's purses and press together tightly to seal right above the pouches of fruit. Separate the layers of filo at the top of the purses and gently fan out. Place the purses on a parchment-lined sheet pan and bake at 350 degrees for 25 to 30 minutes, or until golden brown.

To make the apples: Cook the remaining 1/2 cup of granulated sugar with the water in a small, heavy-bottomed sauté pan over medium heat for 5 minutes, or until golden brown and caramelized. Add the apples and continue to cook for 5 minutes, or until the apples are soft.

ASSEMBLY Spoon some of the warm apple mixture in the center of each plate and spoon some of the Caramel–Kaffir Lime Sauce over the apples and around the plates. Top with a beggar's purse. Sprinkle the kaffir leaves around the plates and place a small scoop of Mamey Sapote Ice Cream on top of each beggar's purse.

Caramel–Kaffir Lime Sauce

Yield: approximately 3/4 cup

3/4 cup sugar

1/4 cup water

1/4 cup freshly squeezed lime juice

3 kaffir lime leaves, coarsely chopped

METHOD Cook the sugar and water in a small, heavy-bottomed sauté pan over medium heat for 5 minutes, or until golden brown and caramelized. Add the lime juice and kaffir leaves and bring to a boil. Strain through a fine-mesh sieve. Warm just prior to serving. Thin with more lime juice if the sauce is too thick.

Mamey Sapote Ice Cream

Yield: 3 cups

2 cups heavy cream

4 egg yolks

1/4 cup sugar

3/4 cup mamey sapote purée

METHOD Bring the cream to a boil. Whisk together the egg yolks and sugar and slowly pour in some of the hot cream. Pour the egg mixture into the cream and cook for 2 to 3 minutes, or until the mixture coats the back of a spoon and steam rises from the top. Cool over an ice water bath, stirring occasionally, until chilled. Mix in the mamey sapote purée and strain through a fine-mesh sieve. Freeze in an ice cream machine and keep frozen until ready to use.

Mango Compote with
Green Tea Crème Brûlée Tart
and Black Sapote Sauce

*This green tea custard can be baked in a brûlée mold or in a tart shell if more substance is desired.
With the mango and the heady, almost seductive black sapote sauce, this preparation
practically pulsates with lushness. Black sapote is not easy to find, but tropical fruit suppliers
do come across it from time to time. There's really nothing quite like it, but an intense,
coffee-flavored anglaise, a purée of lychee nuts, or even white sapote could be substituted.
You can also spice up the mangoes with roasted chile pieces for another interesting variation.*

Serves 6

Cream Cheese Dough (see Appendices)

1 1/2 cups heavy cream

2 teaspoons green tea

4 egg yolks

1/2 cup plus 1 tablespoon sugar

2 ripe black sapote

3/4 cup Simple Syrup (see Appendices)

1/2 cup freshly squeezed lime juice

2 mangoes, peeled, pitted, and thinly sliced

METHOD To make the tart shells: Place six 3-inch-diameter by 1/2-inch-high tart rings on a parchment-lined sheet pan. Roll the Cream Cheese Dough out to 1/8 inch thick. Cut six 4-inch circles and press into the rings. Refrigerate for 30 minutes. Trim the excess dough from the tarts and prick the bottoms with a fork. Line the tarts with parchment paper and weight them down with pastry weights or dried beans. Bake at 350 degrees for 15 to 20 minutes, or until the pastry is set. Remove the weights and the parchment and return the tart shells to the oven for an additional 5 to 10 minutes, or until the crust is golden brown and cooked all the way through.

To make the custard: Prepare an ice water bath. Bring the cream and green tea to a boil. Whisk together the egg yolks and 6 tablespoons of the sugar and slowly pour in some of the hot cream to temper the eggs. Pour the eggs into the cream mixture and place on top of a double boiler over barely simmering water. Stir continuously for 25 minutes, or until very thick. Cool in the ice water bath, stirring occasionally. Spoon the custard into the tart shells and smooth the tops.

To make the sauce: Peel and seed the black sapote (you should have about 1 cup). Purée the sapote, 1/4 cup of the Simple Syrup, and 1/4 cup of the lime juice for 2 minutes, or until smooth. Strain through a fine-mesh sieve. If necessary, thin with a little water to a sauce consistency.

To prepare the mangoes: Warm the mango slices in the remaining 1/2 cup Simple Syrup and 1/4 cup lime juice just prior to serving.

ASSEMBLY Sprinkle the remaining 3 tablespoons sugar over the custard tarts and heat with a blowtorch for 10 seconds, or until caramelized. Arrange some of the mango slices in the center of each plate. Top with a tart and drizzle the black sapote sauce around the plates.

Banana Financier with Milk Chocolate Ice Cream

Bananas and chocolate are one of the all-time great flavor combinations, and that point is proven dramatically with this dessert. The warm, moist cake with buttery, hazelnut overtones superbly highlights the lightly glazed banana pieces, and the strip of oven-dried banana adds a wonderful, chewy texture and a concentrated flavor. The mild-flavored ice cream sits atop everything, contributing an indulgent creaminess.

Serves 6

1/2 cup unsalted butter

Pulp and pod of 1/2 vanilla bean

3 egg whites

1 1/2 cups plus 1 tablespoon confectioners' sugar

1/2 cup plus 2 1/2 tablespoons flour

1 3/4 ounces hazelnuts, toasted, loose skins removed, and ground

2 bananas, peeled and thinly sliced

2 tablespoons granulated sugar

Oven-Dried Banana Rings (recipe follows)

Milk Chocolate Ice Cream (see Appendices)

METHOD To make the cake: Brown the butter with the vanilla pulp and bean for 5 minutes, or until the butter is dark brown and has a nutty aroma. Remove the vanilla bean and let the butter cool. Whisk the egg whites to soft peaks, gradually add the confectioners' sugar, and whisk until tripled in volume.

Fold in the flour and nuts and then stir in the browned butter until well combined.

Place 6 lightly oiled 2 1/2-inch-diameter by 1 1/2-inch-high ring molds on a parchment-lined sheet pan. Fill the molds about half full with the batter and bake at 350 degrees for 15 minutes, or until a toothpick inserted in the center comes out clean. Cool, remove the ring molds, and trim off the tops of the cakes to make them 1 inch high. Arrange the banana slices on the top of the cakes and sprinkle with the sugar. Using a blow-torch, caramelize the sugar on each cake for 30 seconds, or until golden brown.

ASSEMBLY Place a cake in the center of each plate. Place an Oven-Dried Banana Ring around each cake and top with a quenelle of Milk Chocolate Ice Cream.

Oven-Dried Banana Rings

Yield: 6 rings

3 firm bananas, peeled

3 to 4 tablespoons sugar

METHOD Slice the bananas lengthwise, as thinly as possible, with a mandoline. Lay the slices on a Silpat-lined or nonstick sheet pan side by side and end to end, with the edges just overlapping. Sprinkle the bananas with the sugar and bake at 225 degrees for 40 to 60 minutes, or until dry to the touch. Using a pizza cutter or sharp knife, cut the bananas into strips 1 inch wide and long enough to wrap around the ring molds with a slight overlap (about 8 inches long). Return the strips to the oven and continue drying, removing them when they are dry yet still pliable enough to bend. Remove from the oven and loosely wrap around the molds to form rings. Lift away the molds and cool banana rings before using.

Tree Fruits

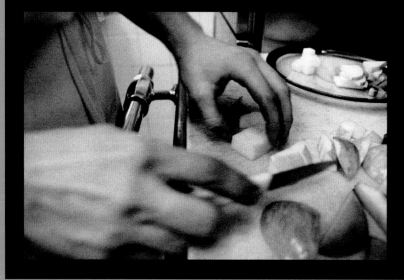

Tree fruits automatically bring to mind the many styles of Loire Valley wines. Chenin Blanc grapes, the glory of the Loire Valley, provide some of the best and most diverse styles of sweet wine. Many of them exhibit apple, pear, and peach flavors acquired from fruit trees that grow nearby, or even in the vineyards. The vibrantly sweet flavors of the wines from Coteaux de Layon, or the slightly more acidic elegance of Bonnezeaux or Quarts de Chaume are all magnificent matches with pears and apples. Vouvray produces a long-aging Moelleux-style wine that displays delicious apple and pear flavors in its youth, then develops rich, dry, peachy flavors with age. Other good choices are the incredibly sweet Beerenauslese and Trockenbeerenauslese wines from Austria's Neusiedlersee. Grapes such as Scheurebe, Welschriesling, and Chardonnay are intense with apple and peach flavors, and naturally high in acidity for a clean finish, qualifying them as good matches for rich fruit desserts.  For prevalent pear flavor the incredibly rare yet gratifying Recolte Tardive Condrieu, from Yves Cuilleron, will send your palate into overdrive.

Elephant Heart Plum Roulade with
Plum Compote and Pistachio Emulsion

This is a very refined, feminine dessert. The flavors and textures exquisitely meld, with the pistachio notes perfectly complementing the plum. This is another great dish to make ahead of time. The sponge cake and filling can be made the day before and then assembled six to eight hours in advance of serving. Peaches or apricots can easily be substituted for the plums, and, for a little extra zest, try adding some Preserved Ginger to the filling.

Serves 8

13 ripe Elephant Heart plums, peeled, pitted, and sliced

³/₄ cup Simple Syrup (see Appendices)

¹/₄ cup heavy cream

¹/₂ cup mascarpone

1 tablespoon sugar

Sponge Cake (recipe follows)

¹/₄ cup chopped pistachios

Pistachio Emulsion (recipe follows)

METHOD To make the filling and the compote: Cook the plums in the Simple Syrup and enough water to cover for 15 minutes, or until the slices are tender. (The plums will have broken down slightly and only a small amount of the syrup will remain.) Remove from the heat and let cool. Whip the cream to soft peaks, add the mascarpone and sugar, and whip until stiff peaks form. Fold in about half of the plum compote.

To assemble the roulade: Turn out the Sponge Cake on a sheet of plastic wrap. Remove the parchment paper and spoon the plum-cream mixture along the long side of the cake. Spoon about one-third of the cooked plum slices on top of the cream and roll tightly, using the plastic wrap to help pull it tight. Wrap the roll in the plastic wrap and refrigerate for at least 30 minutes.

ASSEMBLY Cut the roulade in sixteen ¹/₂-inch slices. Spoon some of the remaining warm plum slices in the center of each plate. Top with 2 roulade slices and sprinkle with a few chopped pistachios. Spoon the Pistachio Emulsion around the plate.

Sponge Cake

Yield: one 9 by 13-inch cake

2 tablespoons milk

1 tablespoon unsalted butter

6 tablespoons sugar

2 eggs

1 egg yolk

6 tablespoons flour, sifted

¹/₂ teaspoon baking powder

METHOD Heat the milk and butter until warm. Whisk together the sugar, eggs, and egg yolk in a metal bowl and place over barely simmering water for 5 minutes, or until the sugar is dissolved. Remove from the heat and whip with an electric mixer on high speed for 5 minutes, or until tripled in volume. Fold in the flour and baking powder until combined. Add the warm milk mixture and fold until just combined. Spread the batter into a parchment-lined and buttered 9 by 13-inch pan. Bake at 400 degrees for 10 minutes, or until light golden brown, and let cool in the pan.

Pistachio Emulsion

Yield: approximately 2 cups

¹/₂ cup firmly packed spinach leaves

³/₄ cup milk

2 tablespoons sugar

2 tablespoons toasted pistachios

¹/₂ teaspoon lime zest

METHOD Blanch the spinach leaves, shock in ice water, squeeze out any excess water, and coarsely chop. Cook the milk, sugar, and pistachios over medium heat for 5 minutes, or until simmering. Pour into a blender, add the lime zest and spinach, and purée for 2 minutes, or until smooth. Strain through a fine-mesh sieve and mix with a handheld blender until frothy.

Poached Pears Wrapped in Brioche with Armagnac-Prune Ice Cream and Prune Sauce

This brioche-wrapped pear truly tops the comfort-food scale. The pear is delicately poached through, filled with an intense, aromatic mixture of prune and almond praline, then wrapped in the rich pastry. Puff pastry or filo can be substituted for the brioche, but the brioche offers the most earthy and satisfying results because of its slight chewiness. A prune-laden Armagnac ice cream brings the tones of the pear, prune, and almond together in perfect harmony. Vanilla ice cream can be substituted for the Armagnac-Prune Ice Cream, and a little Armagnac can be incorporated into the sauce for similar results with a little less work. The pear can be served hot out of the oven or cooled to room temperature. The ingredients are enough to serve 8 if you simply use 8 small pears in place of the 4 standard-size ones.

Serves 4

4 large semiripe pears, peeled

1 cup Sauternes

Pulp and pod of 1 vanilla bean

¼ cup freshly squeezed lemon juice

1 cup chopped pitted dried prunes

½ cup Almond Praline (see Appendices)

¼ cup crème fraîche

Brioche Dough, refrigerated for 3 hours (see Appendices)

1 egg, beaten

½ cup sugar

½ cup freshly squeezed orange juice

⅛ teaspoon ground cinnamon

Armagnac-Prune Ice Cream (recipe follows)

METHOD To make the pears: Scoop out the core and part of the flesh from the bottom of the pears. Place the pears in a medium roasting pan with the Sauternes, vanilla pulp and pod, lemon juice, and enough water to cover the pears. Simmer for 20 minutes, or until the tip of a sharp knife inserted into a pear slides out easily. Remove the pears from the liquid and set upright on a towel to cool and drain.

To make the filling: Combine ½ cup of the prunes, the Almond Praline, and crème fraîche and spoon it into the cavities of the cooled pears.

To wrap the pears: Roll out the Brioche Dough to ⅛ inch thick and cut into circles large enough to cover the pears (approximately 6 to 8 inches in diameter). Poke the pear stem through the center of the brioche and drape the brioche around the pear, smoothing it to form an even layer around the pear. Cut off any excess dough from the bottom and pinch the edges together to make a tight seal. Place the pears on a parchment-lined sheet pan and refrigerate for 30 minutes. Brush the brioche with the egg and roll in the sugar to coat the entire pear. Place the pears upright on a sheet pan and bake at 325 degrees for 15 minutes, or until the brioche is light golden brown and fully cooked.

To make the sauce: Combine the remaining ½ cup prunes, the orange juice, and cinnamon in a food processor and pulse until slightly chunky. Warm just before serving.

ASSEMBLY Spoon approximately ¼ cup of the warm prune sauce in the center of each plate. Cut each of the pears in half lengthwise and place 2 halves upright on each plate. Place a quenelle of Armagnac-Prune Ice Cream next to the pears.

Armagnac-Prune Ice Cream

Yield: approximately 3 cups

1 cup Armagnac

¼ cup chopped pitted prunes

2 cups heavy cream

4 egg yolks

¼ cup sugar

METHOD Simmer the Armagnac over medium heat for 20 minutes or until reduced to about ½ cup. Add the prunes and set aside for 30 minutes.

Prepare an ice water bath. Bring the cream to a boil. Whisk together the egg yolks and sugar and slowly pour in some of the hot cream to temper the yolks. Pour the eggs into the cream and cook for 2 to 3 minutes, or until the mixture coats the back of a spoon and steam rises from the top. Strain through a fine-mesh sieve. Cool over an ice water bath, stirring occasionally, until chilled. Remove the prunes from the Armagnac and reserve. Add the Armagnac to the cream mixture and stir until combined. Freeze in an ice cream machine, adding the prunes just before the ice cream is frozen. Keep frozen until ready to use.

Comfort me with apples, for I am sick of love. –The Song of Solomon 2:4

Forelle Pears with Medjool Dates and Quinoa Tuiles

This dessert is incredibly light, and it explodes with flavor and texture. The meltaway, vanilla-flavored pears; crispy, nutty, quinoa tuiles; meaty, exotic Medjool dates; and the satiny, heady Pear-Cognac Anglaise harmonize beautifully. This dish would make a splendid first course in a dessert progression. For a more elegant presentation the tuiles can be left flat, the pears can be thinly sliced, and the components can be layered with the anglaise to create a napoleon.

Serves 6

9 Forelle pears, peeled, cored, and quartered
1 cup Simple Syrup (see Appendices)
1/2 cup freshly squeezed lemon juice
Pulp and pod of 1 vanilla bean
6 Medjool dates, julienned, plus 3 chopped
1/3 cup freshly squeezed orange juice
1/4 cup water
Quinoa Lace Tuiles (recipe follows)
Pear-Cognac Anglaise (recipe follows)

METHOD To make the pears: Cook the pears with the Simple Syrup, lemon juice, and vanilla pulp and pod over medium heat for 10 minutes, or until tender.

To prepare the dates: Cook the julienned dates in the orange juice until just warm. Remove the dates and reserve the juice. Dice 2 tablespoons of the dates for garnish.

To make the date purée: Place the 3 chopped dates in a blender with the water and the reserved orange juice. Purée for 3 minutes, or until smooth.

ASSEMBLY Arrange equal amounts of the pears, julienned dates, and Quinoa Lace Tuiles on each plate. Sprinkle some of the diced dates on the plates and drizzle with the date purée. Spoon the froth from the top of the Pear-Cognac Anglaise around the plate.

Quinoa Lace Tuiles

Yield: 1 cup batter

1/2 cup unsalted butter, softened
3/4 cup sugar
1 tablespoon honey
1 tablespoon brandy
3 tablespoons plus 1 teaspoon quinoa flour
2 tablespoons all-purpose flour
Pinch of salt

METHOD Combine the butter and sugar with a fork. Add the honey, brandy, flours, and salt and stir until smooth. Drop 3/4 to 1 teaspoon of the batter onto a Silpat-lined or nonstick sheet pan and spread into a thin circle. Repeat until you have at least 12 tuiles. Bake at 350 degrees for 10 minutes, or until golden brown. Cut each circle in half, twist slightly while still hot, and remove to the counter to cool. (If the tuiles harden too quickly, they can be returned to the oven to soften.)

Pear-Cognac Anglaise

Yield: approximately 3/4 cup

1/4 cup sugar
1/2 cup cream
1/2 ripe pear, peeled, cored, and diced
2 tablespoons Cognac

METHOD Dissolve the sugar in the cream over medium heat. Add the pear and simmer for 4 to 5 minutes, or until the pear is softened. Purée the mixture and strain through a fine-mesh sieve. Stir in the Cognac. Reblend just before serving to create a frothy head.

A Study in Lady Apples

*Each of the three parts of this dish would make a great dessert on its own, but featuring
all three creates an absolutely stunning effect. These components provide distinct flavor
and textural contrasts, but they are also light and healthful, which never hurts.
All you need to send this dessert right over the top is a glass of old Calvados.*

Serves 4

*Mascarpone and Black Walnut Praline–
Stuffed Lady Apple (recipe follows)*

Apple Tarte Tatin (recipe follows)

Lady Apple Tuiles (recipe follows)

*Apple-Butterscotch Ice Cream
(recipe follows)*

Clear Lady Apple Chips (see Appendices)

Apple Granité (recipe follows)

Apple-Caramel Sauce (recipe follows)

ASSEMBLY Place a warm Mascarpone and
Black Walnut Praline–Stuffed Lady Apple
in the center of each plate. To the left, place
a warm Apple Tarte Tatin and lay a Lady
Apple Tuile on top. Place a quenelle of
Apple-Butterscotch Ice Cream on top of the
tuile. To the right of the stuffed apple, layer
the Clear Lady Apple Chips and the Apple
Granité, creating an apple shape by pro-
gressing from small, to medium, then
large, then medium, and finally small
apple chips. You will have 4 layers of granité, ending with a final apple chip. Spoon
the Apple-Caramel Sauce around the plate.

Mascarpone and Black Walnut Praline–Stuffed Lady Apples

Yield: 4 stuffed apples

½ cup mascarpone

1 egg yolk

1 tablespoon Simple Syrup (see Appendices)

*½ cup Black Walnut Praline
(see Appendices)*

4 lady apples

METHOD Whisk together the mascarpone,
egg yolk, and Simple Syrup until completely
combined and fold in the Black Walnut
Praline. Refrigerate until ready to use.

Cut out the stem and core of the apples,
leaving the bottoms intact. Use a small
spoon to form a cavity in the apples. Place
the apples on a parchment-lined sheet pan
and bake at 375 degrees for 15 to 20 minutes, or until they soften slightly. Fill the
apples with the chilled mascarpone mixture and bake for an additional 15 to 20
minutes, or until the apples are tender.
Serve immediately.

Apple Tarte Tatin

Yield: 4 tartes

1 to 2 lady apples, peeled

*½ recipe Cream Cheese Dough
(see Appendices)*

*3 tablespoons Apple-Caramel Sauce
(recipe follows)*

METHOD Cut the apples vertically along
the outside of the core and then cut them
crosswise into eight ¼-inch-thick half-
circles. Lay the slices on the work surface to
form 4 circles and use a ring cutter to cut
them into 1½-inch circles. Roll out the
dough on a lightly floured surface to ¼
inch thick and cut four 1½-inch discs.
Refrigerate the dough and the apples until
ready to use.

Wrap the bottom and lower two-thirds of
four 1½-inch-diameter ring cutters or ring
molds with aluminum foil and pour in
enough of the Apple-Caramel Sauce to just
coat the bottom. Lay 2 pieces of lady apple
side by side in the base of each mold and
place a disc of dough on top of the apples.
Refrigerate for about 15 minutes and then
bake at 375 degrees for 15 to 20 minutes, or
until golden brown. Remove the tartes from
the oven and run a small knife around the
edges of the mold to loosen the tarte. Invert
the tartes onto a plate and remove the molds.

Lady Apple Tuiles

Yield: approximately 1 cup batter

1 cup peeled, chopped lady apples

1 egg white

1 tablespoon freshly squeezed lemon juice

2 tablespoons sugar

⅛ teaspoon ground cinnamon

METHOD Place the apple, egg white, and
lemon juice in a blender and purée for 2

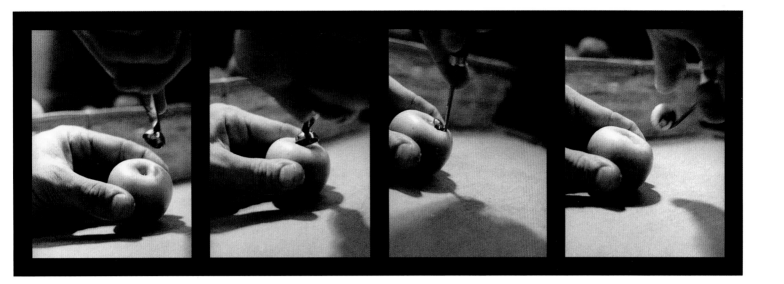

minutes, or until the apple is very smooth. Using an offset spatula, spread the batter on a Silpat-lined or nonstick sheet pan in 2½ by 1½-inch rectangles. Combine the sugar and cinnamon and sprinkle the mixture on the tuiles. Bake at 225 degrees for 20 to 30 minutes, or until thoroughly dry. Carefully remove the tuiles from the pan while still warm and bend them slightly. If the tuiles stick to the Silpat, return them to the oven to soften. Cool and keep in an airtight container at room temperature until ready to use.

Apple-Butterscotch Ice Cream

Yield: approximately 3 cups

¼ cup firmly packed brown sugar
2 tablespoons water
1½ tablespoons unsalted butter
2 cups plus 1 tablespoon heavy cream
1 cup apple juice
1 cup peeled, chopped lady apples
3 egg yolks
2 tablespoons sugar

METHOD To make the butterscotch: Melt the brown sugar and water in a small, heavy-bottomed sauté pan over medium heat. Cook for 5 minutes, or until the sugar has caramelized and thickened. Add the butter and 1 tablespoon of the cream, carefully whisk together, and remove from the heat.

Cook the apple juice over medium-high heat for 20 to 30 minutes, or until reduced

to ¼ cup. Prepare an ice water bath. Bring the remaining 2 cups of cream and the apple to a boil. Whisk together the egg yolks and sugar. Slowly pour in some of the hot cream mixture to temper the eggs and whisk in the reduced apple juice. Pour the egg mixture into the cream and continue to cook, stirring continuously for 2 to 3 minutes, or until the mixture coats the back of a spoon and steam rises from the top. Remove from the heat and strain through a fine-mesh sieve, reserving the apples. Purée the apples and ½ cup of the custard until smooth. Pour the apple mixture into the custard and let cool in the ice water bath, stirring occasionally, until chilled. Freeze in an ice cream machine. Before the ice cream has completely set, fold in the butterscotch. Keep frozen until ready to use.

Apple Granité

Yield: 2 cups

3 cups peeled, chopped lady apples
¼ cup freshly squeezed lemon juice
¼ cup Simple Syrup (see Appendices)

METHOD Pureé the apples and lemon juice for 2 minutes, or until smooth, and strain through a fine-mesh sieve. Add the Simple Syrup and whisk until thoroughly combined. Pour into a shallow container, cover, and place in the freezer. To form the granité, scrape the mixture with a spoon every 15 to 20 minutes for 2 hours, or until frozen. Keep frozen until ready to use.

Apple-Caramel Sauce

Yield: ½ cup

½ cup sugar
¼ cup water
¼ cup warm apple juice

METHOD Cook the sugar and water in a small, heavy-bottomed sauté pan over medium heat for 5 minutes, or until golden brown. Add the apple juice and continue to cook for 3 minutes. Remove from the heat and let cool slightly. Thin to a sauce consistency with apple juice, if necessary. Serve warm.

Quince Crisp with Buttermilk-Pineapple Sherbet

This crisp seems rich, but it is really quite light and full of flavor.
And it's surprisingly simple to make. You can serve this molded, as I have,
or serve it in a single-serving ceramic or porcelain dish for a more casual meal.
Other fruits, such as apples, pears, or pineapple, can easily be substituted for the quince.
If a richer dessert is desired, vanilla ice cream can be used in place of this lean,
almost poetic sherbet.

Serves 6

½ cup sugar

½ cup unsalted butter, diced

½ cup flour

¼ cup cornmeal

½ teaspoon chopped fresh thyme

1 large quince, peeled and cut into small dice (about 1½ cups)

1 cup water

2 tablespoons freshly squeezed lemon juice

2 tablespoons crème fraîche

Buttermilk-Pineapple Sherbet (recipe follows)

METHOD To make the streusel: Combine ¼ cup of the sugar, the butter, flour, cornmeal, and thyme in a food processor, pulsing until crumbly. Spread the mixture on a sheet pan and bake at 325 degrees for 25 minutes, or until golden brown. (The mixture will seem to break down and then brown.) Let cool slightly and then crumble into small pieces.

To prepare the quince: Cook the quince, water, lemon juice, and the remaining ¼ cup of sugar over medium heat, stirring continuously, until the water evaporates and the sugar begins to turn light golden brown and caramelize. If the quince is not fully cooked, add an additional ¼ cup water and continue to cook. Remove from the heat, add the crème fraîche, and mix thoroughly.

ASSEMBLY Place a 2½ by 2½-inch mold (or other similar size mold) in the center of each plate. Divide the quince mixture between the 6 molds and top with about 2 tablespoons of the streusel mixture, pressing down firmly on the streusel. Remove the mold and top with a quenelle of Buttermilk-Pineapple Sherbet.

Buttermilk-Pineapple Sherbet

Yield: 1 quart

2¼ cups unsweetened pineapple juice

1½ cups buttermilk

1 cup Simple Syrup (see Appendices)

3 tablespoons corn syrup

METHOD Combine all of the ingredients and refrigerate to chill. Freeze in an ice cream machine and keep frozen until ready to use.

Black Mission Fig Terrine with Israeli Couscous Sauce

This terrine may look difficult to make, but it is actually quite simple.
A little gelatin combined with Port and fig juices creates a wonderful, light binding agent.
After the terrine is sliced, crispy oven-dried figs are adhered to the edges to add a
fascinating textural element, and the creamy sauce, made from Israeli couscous and orange juice,
supplies a satisfying earthiness. This light, healthful dessert could also be prepared
with apricots, peaches, or other fruits.

Serves 8

³/₄ cup plus 2 tablespoons sugar

³/₄ cup water

¹/₂ cup Port, warmed

20 fresh Black Mission figs, quartered

5 sheets gelatin

¹/₄ cup Israeli couscous

¹/₄ cup freshly squeezed orange juice

Oven-Dried Fig Chips (recipe follows)

White Pepper–Buttermilk Ice Cream (recipe follows)

METHOD To make the terrine: Cook ³/₄ cup of the sugar and ¹/₄ cup of the water in a small, heavy-bottomed sauté pan for 5 to 10 minutes, or until golden brown and caramelized. Add the Port and bring to a boil. Add the figs and stir until slightly softened. Remove from the heat and let cool. Strain in a sieve, reserving the figs and juice separately. If there is less than ¹/₂ cup of juice, add water to bring it up to ¹/₂ cup.

Soften the gelatin in a shallow pan with enough cold water to cover it. Warm half of the juice from the figs. Remove the gelatin from the water and squeeze to remove excess water. Add the gelatin to the warmed fig juice and stir until completely dissolved. Pour the mixture over the figs and let them soak for 5 minutes, tossing occasionally.

Lightly oil a 2¹/₄-inch-wide by 1¹/₂-inch-high by 8-inch-long terrine mold and line with plastic wrap. Layer the figs in the mold, applying some pressure to pack them down. Cover with plastic wrap and refrigerate for at least 1 hour.

To make the fig sauce: Pour the remaining reserved fig juice into a small saucepan and warm. Reduce to thicken to a coating consistency, if necessary.

To make the couscous sauce: Bring the couscous, the remaining ¹/₂ cup water and 2 tablespoons sugar, and the orange juice to a boil. Simmer for 20 minutes, or until the couscous is tender. Add additional water to thin to a sauce consistency, if necessary.

ASSEMBLY Cut into ¹/₂-inch slices and remove the plastic wrap from the slices. Spoon some of the fig sauce in the center of each plate and top with a slice of the terrine. Gently press the Oven-Dried Fig Chips around the edges of the terrine, overlapping them slightly. Spoon the Israeli Couscous Sauce around the plate and place a quenelle of White Pepper–Buttermilk Ice Cream on the sauce.

Oven-Dried Fig Chips

6 fresh Black Mission figs
1 tablespoon sugar

METHOD Cut the figs in half lengthwise and then cut crosswise into ¹/₈-inch-thick or smaller slices. Lay the slices on a Silpat-lined or nonstick sheet pan and sprinkle with the sugar. Bake at 225 degrees for 30 minutes, or until dry. Remove the chips to a countertop or other flat surface to cool.

White Pepper–Buttermilk Ice Cream

Yield: approximately 1 quart

2 cups heavy cream
1 tablespoon white peppercorns, toasted
2 teaspoons orange zest
5 egg yolks
¹/₂ cup sugar
1¹/₂ cups buttermilk

METHOD Bring the cream, white peppercorns, and orange zest to a boil. Remove from heat, cover, and let steep for 30 minutes. Prepare an ice water bath. Return the cream mixture to the heat and bring to a boil. Whisk together the egg yolks and sugar and slowly pour in some of the hot cream to temper the eggs. Pour the eggs into the cream and continue to cook for 2 to 3 minutes, or until the mixture coats the back of a spoon and steam rises from the top. Strain through a fine-mesh sieve and cool in the ice water bath, stirring occasionally, until chilled. Add the buttermilk and freeze in an ice cream machine. Keep frozen until ready to use.

Black Plum Croustillant with White Chocolate Sabayon

The meltingly soft fruit nestled against the crispy pastry in this tart offers an extraordinary textural contrast, not to mention a soothing delicately sweet plum flavor. The White Chocolate Sabayon is spooned on for a luscious ribbon of sauce. This preparation would also work marvelously with a scoop of vanilla ice cream instead of the sabayon.

Serves 4

8 black plums

5 tablespoons unsalted butter

1/3 cup plus 2 tablespoons sugar

2 egg yolks

1/3 cup milk

1/2 teaspoon pure vanilla extract

1 cup cake flour

1 teaspoon baking powder

1/2 teaspoon baking soda

1/4 teaspoon salt

2 ounces white chocolate, melted and cooled slightly

1 package (170 grams) Feuille de Brick Crepe, cut into twenty 2 1/2-inch circles

White Chocolate Sabayon (recipe follows)

1/2 ounce white chocolate, shaved with a vegetable peeler

METHOD To prepare the plum slices: Cut 1/8-inch vertical slices from 4 of the plums. Cut each slice in half crosswise to form 2 half circles.

To make the croustillants: Cream 3 tablespoons of the butter and 1/3 cup of the sugar. Whisk together the egg yolks, milk, and vanilla extract. Combine the flour, baking powder, baking soda, and salt. Alternate adding liquid and dry ingredients to the butter mixture, mixing well after each addition. Stir in the melted white chocolate until it is completely incorporated. Place 4 circles of Feuille de Brick Crepe on a parchment-lined sheet pan and top each one with 1 teaspoon of batter. Spread the batter, leaving a 1/4-inch border. Continue layering the Feuille de Brick Crepe and batter until there are 5 layers of batter (end with the batter). Repeat this process 3 more times for a total of 4 cakes. Arrange the plum slices on the top, overlapping them slightly and trimming as necessary to resemble the petals of a flower. Refrigerate for 30 minutes. Lightly sprinkle the 4 cakes with 2 to 3 teaspoons of the sugar and bake at 350 degrees for 25 minutes, or until golden brown.

To prepare the plum wedges: Cut the remaining 4 plums into 8 wedges each. Cook the remaining 2 tablespoons butter until it is almost smoking. Add the plum wedges and the remaining 1 tablespoon sugar and cook for 2 to 3 minutes, or until warm. (The skins may come off the plums.)

ASSEMBLY Arrange the plum wedges and some of the cooking juices in the center of each plate and top with a warm plum croustillant. Spoon some of the White Chocolate Sabayon around the plate and sprinkle the sabayon with the shaved white chocolate.

White Chocolate Sabayon

Yield: approximately 1 cup

4 egg yolks

2 tablespoons Simple Syrup (see Appendices)

1 ounce white chocolate, chopped

1/4 cup crème fraîche

METHOD Whisk the egg yolks and Simple Syrup in a double boiler over barely simmering water for 10 minutes, or until it reaches the ribbon stage. Add the chocolate, stir until it is melted, and let cool. Fold in the crème fraîche just prior to serving.

This whimsical, refreshing, and richly satisfying dessert is great for those who want a taste of chocolate at the end of a meal but don't want to be overwhelmed by it. Here, a poached pear is filled with a chocolate custard, which is then caramelized. Pear is placed on a crispy filo cup to add textural variety. Cumin and Almond Praline add interesting flavor and textural notes. The custard can be set in the poached pears a few hours in advance, but not much earlier or the natural juices in the pear will cause the custard to break down. The last-minute assembly goes quickly, though.

ed
sting

ppendices)
ean
on juice
ecipe follows)
gar

Appendices)

cups: Lay out a
one-third of the
kle with confec-
another sheet of
ird of the butter,
s' sugar, and top
rush lightly with
cut the stack into
4 ramekins (or
oan and center a
kin. Press down
to the shape of
nother inverted,
or cup to help it
325 degrees for 5
er ramekin and

continue to bake for 10 minutes, or until golden brown. Remove the filo cup from the ramekin while it is still hot and cool on the counter.

To prepare the pears: Combine the pears, cinnamon sticks, Sauternes, Simple Syrup, vanilla pulp and pod, lemon juice, and enough water to cover the pears in a medium saucepan. Cover with parchment and simmer for 20 to 25 minutes, or until the pears are tender. Remove the pears and reduce the poaching liquid by half. Reserve ½ cup of the reduced liquid. Cut the tops off the pears, leaving a 2-inch-thick base.

To make the dried pear chips: Cut at least 6 very thin slices from the pear tops, cutting close to the stem to get the largest pieces possible. Place on a Silpat-lined or nonstick sheet pan and bake at 225 degrees for 30 minutes, or until the slices are dry and crisp. Dice the remaining pear tops and set aside for the sauce.

To make the stuffed pears: Scoop out the cores and some of the flesh from the base of the pears without going all the way to the bottom. Fill the centers with the chocolate custard and refrigerate for 1 hour. Sprinkle ½ tablespoon of the granulated sugar on top of each pear and heat with a blowtorch for 30 seconds, or until golden brown and caramelized. Immediately place a dried pear chip upright in the center of each pear.

To make the sauce: Dissolve the remaining 1 tablespoon granulated sugar in the reserved ½ cup poaching liquid and keep warm. Cook the butter until it is dark brown and has a nutty aroma. Add the cumin and the diced pears and stir into the syrup.

ASSEMBLY Spoon some of the diced pears and butter sauce on each plate. Spoon about 2 tablespoons of the chocolate custard in the center of each plate. Place an inverted filo cup over the custard and top with a stuffed pear. Sprinkle the Almond Praline around the plate.

Milk Chocolate Custard

Yield: approximately 2 cups

1½ cups heavy cream
3 ounces milk chocolate, chopped
4 egg yolks
1½ tablespoons sugar

METHOD Prepare an ice water bath. Bring the cream to a boil and pour over the chopped chocolate. Whisk the egg yolks and sugar in a double boiler over barely simmering water for 10 minutes, or until doubled in volume. Pour the chocolate into the egg mixture and continue cooking, stirring continuously, for 20 to 30 minutes, or until it reaches a thick custard consistency. Place over the ice water bath, stirring occasionally, for 45 minutes, or until chilled. Refrigerate until ready to use.

Whole Roasted Apricot with Basil Ice Cream and Candied Basil Leaves

~~~~~~

*Serving a dessert in a fruit shell allows you to avoid the richness of pastry
but still enjoy the wonderful flavors of a tart-type filling. The apricots are roasted
to concentrate their flavor and then filled with a mixture of praline and dried fruits.
The filling not only provides a great textural counterpoint to the juicy, fleshy fruit,
but its sweetness nicely balances the slightly astringent apricot. Notes of basil,
by way of a satiny ice cream and candied leaves, lend a delicate, sophisticated fragrance
that elevates this earthy combination of flavors.*

Serves 4

5 fresh apricots, peeled

*1/2 cup plus 1 tablespoon Simple Syrup
(see Appendices)*

2 tablespoons dried cranberries

2 tablespoons dried apricots, chopped

1/4 cup Pine Nut Praline (see Appendices)

2 tablespoons water

Basil Ice Cream (recipe follows)

Candied Basil Leaves (recipe follows)

METHOD To make the apricots: Cut off the stem end of the apricots and use a paring knife to cut around the pit. Use the knife to loosen the pit and pop it out. Cut a small slice off the bottom so the apricot will stand upright. Trim the cavity to allow room for the filling, being careful not to pierce the skin. Toss the apricots in 1/2 cup of the Simple Syrup and bake in a small pan at 375 degrees for 20 minutes, or until tender, basting periodically with more of the Simple Syrup. Transfer the apricots to a plate to cool.

To make the filling: Pour the roasting juices from the apricots into a small saucepan. Add the cranberries to the saucepan and cook until they are soft and plump, adding water if necessary. When the cranberries are plumped and glazed in the syrup, stir in the dried apricots. Remove from the heat, let cool, and then stir in the Pine Nut Praline. Spoon the mixture into 4 of the roasted apricots.

To make the apricot sauce: Place the remaining roasted apricot in a blender with the remaining 1 tablespoon Simple Syrup and the water and purée for 2 minutes, or until smooth. Strain through a fine-mesh sieve.

ASSEMBLY Place a stuffed apricot in the center of each plate and place a quenelle of Basil Ice Cream next to it. Drizzle the apricot sauce and arrange the Candied Basil Leaves around the plate.

Basil Ice Cream

Yield: approximately 3 cups

2 cups heavy cream

1/2 cup firmly packed fresh basil leaves

1 1/2 teaspoons orange zest

4 egg yolks

6 tablespoons sugar

METHOD Bring the cream, 1/4 cup of the basil, and the orange zest to a boil. Remove from the heat, cover, and let steep for 30 minutes. Prepare an ice water bath. Return the cream mixture to the heat and bring to a boil. Whisk together the egg yolks and sugar and slowly pour in some of the hot cream to temper the eggs. Pour the eggs into the cream and continue to cook for 2 to 3 minutes, or until the mixture coats the back of a spoon and steam rises from the top. Cool in the ice water bath, stirring occasionally, until chilled. Pour the mixture into a blender with the remaining 1/4 cup basil and purée for 3 minutes, or until smooth. Strain through a fine-mesh sieve and freeze in an ice cream machine. Keep frozen until ready to use.

Candied Basil Leaves

Yield: 1/4 cup

1/4 cup sugar

2 tablespoons water

1/2 cup fresh basil leaves, chopped

2 tablespoons freshly squeezed orange juice

METHOD Cook the sugar and water in a small, heavy-bottomed sauté pan over medium heat for 5 minutes, or until golden brown. Add the basil and orange juice, stir to dissolve any hardened sugar, and remove from the heat. Place on a Silpat-lined or nonstick sheet pan, separating the basil pieces with two forks. Store in an airtight container at room temperature for up to 2 hours.

Whole Roasted Fig with Goat Cheese Ice Cream, Spicy Fig Sauce, and Oatmeal Tuiles

Figs and goat cheese are natural partners. The creamy, elegant tangy goat cheese perfectly contrasts with the full-flavored figs. In this dessert, a hot roasted fig acts as the bed for a scoop of intoxicatingly perfumed goat cheese ice cream, which melts into the fig to create a perfect sauce. Accompanying the roasted fig is a napoleon featuring crispy oatmeal tuiles layered with raw figs and a sating goat cheese cream. The fig juices and thyme leaves round out the dish nicely.

Serves 6

2 tablespoons unsalted butter

1/4 cup confectioners' sugar

1 1/2 teaspoons finely chopped lemon zest

3 tablespoons honey

1/3 cup flour

3 tablespoons rolled oats, lightly toasted

12 fresh figs

1/2 cup Simple Syrup (see Appendices)

2 tablespoons port

6 tablespoons heavy cream

2 ounces goat cheese

2 tablespoons granulated sugar

Goat Cheese Ice Cream (recipe follows)

Spicy Fig Sauce (recipe follows)

1 tablespoon baby thyme sprigs

METHOD To make the tuiles: Cream the butter, confectioners' sugar, and lemon zest. Add the honey and flour and mix well. Spread about 1/2 teaspoon of the batter onto a Silpat-lined or nonstick sheet pan. Use a small offset spatula to spread the tuile into a 1 3/4-inch circle. Repeat the process, making at least 18 tuiles (the extra will allow for breakage). Sprinkle the top of each tuile with a pinch of rolled oats, reserving 1/2 tablespoon for garnish. Bake at 350 degrees for 5 minutes, or until golden brown. (The tuiles may be cut with a ring cutter after cooking for a more precise shape.) Immediately transfer the tuiles to a countertop or other flat surface to cool.

To prepare the figs: Cut the tops off 6 of the figs. Use a small spoon to press a cavity into each fig and dip the whole fig in the Simple Syrup. Fill the figs with the port. (If the figs have any holes in the bottoms, cut small pieces off the tops to fill the holes.) Place the filled figs on a sheet pan and bake at 350 degrees for 25 minutes, or until they have softened. Slice the remaining 6 figs in half lengthwise and then cut them crosswise into 1/4-inch-thick slices. Warm the slices in the remaining Simple Syrup.

To make the goat cheese cream: Thoroughly combine 2 tablespoons of the heavy cream with the goat cheese and granulated sugar. Whisk the remaining 1/4 cup cream until it reaches soft peaks and fold into the goat cheese mixture.

ASSEMBLY Place 3 to 4 fig slices on one half of each plate. Place a small spoonful of the goat cheese cream on the figs and top with a tuile. Spoon another small spoonful of the cream, 3 to 4 fig slices, another tablespoon of cream, and a tuile on top of the first stack. Build another layer with a spoonful of cream, figs, another spoonful of cream, and a tuile. Place a roasted fig alongside the stacked figs and top with a quenelle of Goat Cheese Ice Cream. Spoon the Spicy Fig Sauce around the plates and sprinkle with the thyme sprigs and the remaining 1/2 tablespoon oatmeal.

Goat Cheese Ice Cream

Yield: approximately 3 cups

2 cups heavy cream

1/2 cup milk

4 egg yolks

1/4 cup sugar

3 tablespoons corn syrup

4 ounces goat cheese

METHOD Prepare an ice water bath. Bring the cream and milk to a boil. Whisk together the egg yolks and sugar and slowly pour in some of the hot cream to temper the eggs. Pour the eggs into the cream and continue to cook for 2 to 3 minutes, or until the mixture coats the back of a spoon and steam rises from the top. Whisk together the corn syrup and goat cheese and then whisk this mixture into the cream mixture until smooth. Strain through a fine-mesh sieve and chill over the ice water bath. Freeze in an ice cream machine. Keep frozen until ready to use.

Spicy Fig Sauce

Yield: 1/2 cup

2 tablespoons sugar

1/4 cup freshly squeezed orange juice, warm

1/2 cup chopped fresh figs

1 star anise

3 whole black peppercorns

METHOD Cook the sugar in a heavy-bottomed sauté pan over medium heat for 3 minutes, or until golden brown. Add the orange juice and bring to a boil. Add the figs, star anise, and peppercorns, bring to a boil, and cook for 3 minutes. Remove from the heat and strain through a fine-mesh sieve, pushing on the solids to remove as much liquid as possible. If necessary, thin with a little warm water to a sauce consistency.

Vegetables & Grains

Winemakers have utilized dried grapes to add sweetness, intensity, complexity, and aging power to their wines almost since winemaking began. Tokaji Aszu from Hungary, Italy's Vin Santo, and the rare, esoteric Vin de Paille from Hermitage or Jura are some of the most rustic, artistic examples of these wines. The few winemakers still producing these wines literally dry the grapes on straw mats, concentrating the flavors to create incredibly intricate wines. These rare wines are some of the oldest styles produced in the world and the nostalgia they evoke is an added bonus. All of these wines offer an earthy complexity that is echoed by the grain, corn, squash, and other vegetables in these desserts. The wines also have a unique caramelized-fruit quality that is the perfect complement to most grain-based desserts.

Israeli Couscous Custard with
Kaffir Lime Sauce and Oven-Dried Strawberries

This fairly simple-to-make rice pudding–like preparation is surprisingly complex in flavor and texture. The toothsome pearls of Israeli couscous suspended in the creamy, delicate custard are a wonderful textural contrast on their own, but when the chewy and intensely concentrated flavor of the Oven-Dried Strawberry Chips is added, the entire dish is elevated to another level. A drizzle of kaffir lime sauce adds an enticingly exotic flavor that weaves all the other flavors together. If you can't find Israeli couscous, basmati rice can be used with similar results. Banana or pineapple can be used in place of the strawberries for a taste variation.

Serves 6

½ cup Israeli couscous

½ cup freshly squeezed orange juice

1 cup water

½ cup sugar

2 sheets gelatin

1 cup plus 2 tablespoons heavy cream

6 tablespoons milk

*6 tablespoons Simple Syrup
(see Appendices)*

1½ tablespoons freshly squeezed lime juice

1 kaffir lime leaf, stem removed and chopped

*Oven-Dried Strawberry Chips
(see Appendices)*

*12 strawberries, scooped into
Parisienne balls*

METHOD To make the custard: Bring the couscous, orange juice, water, and ¼ cup of the sugar to a simmer and cook for 30 minutes, or until the couscous is tender, adding more water if the liquid evaporates before the couscous is tender.

Prepare an ice water bath. Place the gelatin in a shallow bowl, cover with cool water, and let sit until soft. Cook the cream, milk, and remaining ¼ cup of sugar over medium heat for 5 minutes, or until the sugar dissolves. Remove the gelatin from the water, add to the cream, and stir until completely combined. Cool in the ice water bath, stirring occasionally, until chilled.

Fold together the couscous and the cream mixture. Place over the ice water bath and continue to cool, stirring occasionally, until the mixture has thickened enough to keep the couscous evenly distributed in the custard. Spoon into six 2½-inch-diameter by 1½-inch-high lightly oiled ring molds and refrigerate.

To make the lime sauce: Cook the Simple Syrup and lime juice for 5 minutes, or until warm. Pour into a blender, add the kaffir leaf, and purée for 2 minutes.

ASSEMBLY Place a custard-filled ring mold in the center of each plate. Remove the mold and press the Oven-Dried Strawberries onto the sides of the custard. Drizzle the lime sauce around the plate and sprinkle some of the strawberry Parisienne balls on the sauce.

Boniato Custard with Asian Pear, Candied Pomelo, Maple Syrup Tuiles, and Tamarind-Vanilla Sauce

*Boniato is a type of white sweet potato with a sweet, creamy, refined flavor.
Here, a disc of the custard is sandwiched between two lacy maple syrup tuiles, which provide
a fabulous crunchy contrast to the smooth, milky custard. The Asian pears and candied pomelo
add a cleansing note of fresh fruit. The tangy, exotic Tamarind-Vanilla Sauce is the final
coup de grâce of exciting flavor. The true beauty of this preparation is that the custard itself
is not very sweet so the boniato flavor shines through and becomes further enhanced
by the support elements. Most of the components of this dish can be prepared
well in advance, allowing for easy, last-minute assembly.*

Serves 6

1 small boniato, baked until soft
2 cups milk
2 egg yolks
2 eggs
³/4 cup sugar
¹/3 cup freshly squeezed orange juice
¹/2 teaspoon ground cinnamon
2 teaspoons finely chopped lemon zest
2 teaspoons grated fresh ginger
Maple Tuiles (recipe follows)
1 small pomelo
¹/2 cup water
¹/2 cup peeled, shaved Asian pear
Tamarind-Vanilla Sauce (recipe follows)

METHOD To make the custard: Purée the boniato, milk, egg yolks, eggs, ¹/2 cup of the sugar, the orange juice, cinnamon, lemon zest, and ginger for 2 minutes, or until smooth. Strain through a fine-mesh sieve and pour into an 8 by 8-inch pan. Bake in a water bath at 325 degrees for 45 minutes, or until set. Remove from the water bath and refrigerate for 1 hour, or until cool. Cut the custard into 2¹/2-inch circles with a ring mold or cutter, and sandwich between 2 Maple Tuiles.

To make the candied pomelo: Using a vegetable peeler, peel the pomelo in at least ¹/2-inch-wide strips. Cut the strips into ¹/2-inch triangles, blanch in boiling water, drain, and repeat 6 more times. Cook the pomelo triangles in the remaining ¹/4 cup sugar and the water for 20 minutes, or until the liquid has reduced and the peel is candied.

ASSEMBLY Arrange some of the candied pomelo peel and the Asian pear in the center of each plate. Top with a custard sandwich and drizzle the Tamarind-Vanilla Sauce around the plate.

Maple Tuiles

Yield: approximately 12 to 14 tuiles

2 tablespoons unsalted butter
¹/4 cup confectioners' sugar
3 tablespoons pure maple syrup
1 teaspoon honey
¹/3 cup flour

METHOD Cream the butter and confectioners' sugar. Add the maple syrup and honey and mix well. Add the flour and mix until completely combined. Thinly spread the batter on a Silpat-lined or nonstick sheet pan and bake at 350 degrees for 7 to 8 minutes, or until golden brown. Using a lightly oiled cutter, cut into twelve 3-inch circles while still hot. Let the tuiles harden slightly in the pan, and then transfer them to a flat surface to cool.

Tamarind-Vanilla Sauce

Yield: approximately ¹/2 cup

3 pods tamarind, peeled
¹/2 cup freshly squeezed orange juice
¹/4 cup water
Pulp and pod of ¹/2 vanilla bean
¹/4 cup sugar

METHOD Combine all of the ingredients in a small saucepan and bring to a boil. Cover, remove from the heat, and steep for 30 minutes. Remove the vanilla pod and squeeze the tamarind to remove the seeds from the pulp. Blend the mixture slightly with a handheld blender and then strain through a fine-mesh sieve, pushing on the solids to remove as much liquid as possible. Return the liquid to the pan and continue cooking until reduced to ¹/2 cup. Remove from the heat and cool to room temperature.

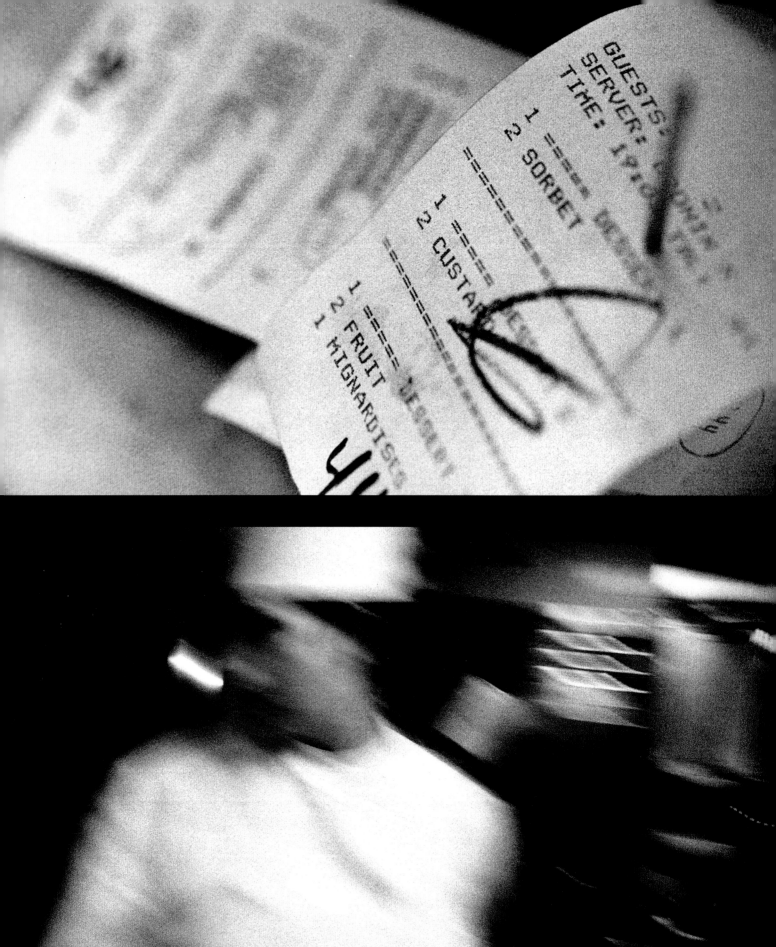

Carrot, Quince and Pine Nut Strudel
with Honey-Chickpea Ice Cream

~~~~~~

The idea for this recipe came from sampling the goods in Arabian pastry shops when I visited Jerusalem. Carrots, with their natural sweetness, work fabulously in many types of desserts, and the chickpeas add a refined starchiness. Here, the ice cream is frozen in a flat pan and then it is cut into squares or circles just before serving. The warm or hot strudel resting on the ice cream makes a glorious temperature contrast. Crispy filo and crunchy Candied Chickpeas provide delightful textural effects. Apple or pineapple can be substituted for the quince with great results.

Serves 4

2 large carrots, cut into batons (about 1 cup)

3 cups water

³/₄ cup sugar

¹/₂ cup dried chickpeas, soaked overnight in water and drained

1 quince, cut into large batons (about 1 cup)

¹/₄ teaspoon ground cinnamon

¹/₄ cup Pine Nut Praline (see Appendices)

¹/₄ cup crème fraîche

¹/₄ cup firmly packed brown sugar

¹/₂ cup unsalted butter, melted

¹/₄ cup honey

4 sheets filo dough

*Honey-Chickpea Ice Cream
(see Appendices)*

Carrot-Honey Sauce (recipe follows)

Candied Chickpeas (recipe follows)

METHOD To make the filling: Cook the carrots, 2 cups of the water, and ¹/₄ cup of the sugar for 10 to 15 minutes, or until the carrots are tender. Remove the carrots from the pan, reserving both the cooking liquid and the carrots. Add the remaining 1 cup water and the chickpeas to the carrot cooking liquid and cook over medium heat for 1¹/₂ to 2 hours, or until the beans are soft (add more water as necessary to keep the beans covered).

Toss the quince with the cinnamon and the remaining ¹/₂ cup sugar. Place on a parchment-lined sheet pan and roast in the oven at 350 degrees, tossing occasionally, for 20 to 30 minutes, or until tender. Allow the carrots, chickpeas, and quince to cool, then fold them together with the Pine Nut Praline, crème fraîche, and brown sugar.

To assemble the strudel: Combine the melted butter and honey in a small bowl. Lay out a sheet of filo on the work surface and brush with the honey mixture. Cover with another sheet of filo and brush with the honey mixture. Cut the layered filo into two 8 by 12-inch sheets. Cover with plastic wrap and set aside. Repeat the process with the 2 remaining sheets of filo. Place one-quarter of the filling along the 8-inch side of both stacks of filo and roll tightly into a log shape, pushing the filling in from both ends to keep the roll well filled. Pinch the ends of the rolls, forcing the filling toward the center, and seal the ends. Cover each roll in plastic wrap and refrigerate for 30 minutes. Remove the plastic wrap, place the rolls on a parchment-lined sheet pan, and brush with the remaining honey-butter mixture. Bake at 350 degrees for 30 minutes, or until golden brown, turning occasionally to ensure even browning. Remove from the oven and let cool for 5 minutes. Trim the rough ends off each roll, then slice the rolls in half on the diagonal.

ASSEMBLY Place a square of Honey-Chickpea Ice Cream on each plate. Stand one of the rolls on one corner of the ice cream and lay another roll behind it. Spoon the Carrot-Honey Sauce around the plate and sprinkle the Candied Chick Peas around the ice cream.

Carrot-Honey Sauce

Yield: ¹/₃ cup

¹/₄ cup honey
2 tablespoons orange zest
1 cup freshly squeezed carrot juice

METHOD Bring the honey and orange zest to a boil and then simmer for 5 minutes, or until golden brown. Add the carrot juice and continue to cook for 15 minutes, or until slightly syrupy. Strain through a fine-mesh sieve and let cool.

Candied Chickpeas

Yield: ¹/₂ cup

¹/₄ cup cooked chickpeas
¹/₄ cup sugar
2 tablespoons water

METHOD Place the chickpeas on a sheet pan. Bake at 300 degrees for 20 minutes, or until the beans start to look dry. Remove the beans from the oven and set aside.

Cook the sugar and water in a small, heavy-bottomed sauté pan over medium-high heat for 7 minutes, or until the sugar turns golden brown. Remove from the heat. Add a few beans at a time to the pan and stir to coat with the sugar mixture. Remove the beans from the pan individually with a fork, draining any excess caramel, and place on a nonstick sheet pan to cool. Repeat until there are at least 32 candied beans. Store in an airtight container at room temperature until needed.

Basmati Rice–Corn Custard with Brazil Nut Crust

This dessert combines the glories of rice pudding and crème brûlée to offer up the best of both. The result is homey yet refined. The Brazil nuts contribute a crunch and match the nutty character of the basmati rice. The corn kernels and dates accentuate the sweetness of the custard while providing an interesting meatiness of their own. Both the custard and the rice pudding mixture sit on a marvelously crunchy, buttery Brazil nut crust. Finally, a luscious, satisfying brown butter sauce is drizzled around the plate, literally linking all the elements.

Serves 6

½ cup basmati rice, rinsed

2 cups milk

½ cup plus 2 tablespoons sugar

2 teaspoons chopped orange zest

¼ cup mascarpone

8 fresh dates, pitted and chopped

½ cup cooked corn

2 egg yolks

¾ cup plus 2 tablespoons heavy cream

⅔ cup Brazil nuts, toasted and loose skins rubbed off

2 tablespoons water

1 tablespoon unsalted butter, melted

Corn Sauce (recipe follows)

Brown Butter–Corn Sauce (recipe follows)

METHOD To make the rice: Cook the rice, milk, 2 tablespoons of the sugar, and the orange zest in a covered pan over low heat for 25 minutes, or until the rice is tender. Remove from the heat and fold in the mascarpone, dates, and corn.

To make the custard: Whisk together the egg yolks and 2 tablespoons of the sugar in a metal bowl over barely simmering water for 7 to 8 minutes, or until doubled in volume. Pour in the cream and continue cooking, stirring continuously, for 20 minutes, or until thickened to a custard consistency. Prepare an ice water bath. Strain through a fine-mesh sieve and cool over the ice water bath, stirring occasionally, until chilled.

To make the crust: Using a vegetable peeler, thinly shave 6 of the Brazil nuts and set aside for garnish. Coarsely chop the remaining nuts. Combine ¼ cup of the sugar and the water in a small, heavy-bottomed sauté pan over medium-high heat. Cook for 10 minutes, or until golden brown and caramelized. Add the chopped nuts, stirring until well coated. If the caramel hardens around the nuts, stir over low heat to dissolve. Pour the nut mixture onto a Silpat-lined or nonstick sheet pan and let cool, then break into pieces. Pulse in a food processor, leaving the mixture fairly chunky. Place the melted butter and the nut mixture in a small bowl and stir until combined.

To assemble the custards: Lightly oil the inside of six 2½-inch-diameter by 1½-inch-high ring molds and place on a parchment-lined sheet pan. Pat about 1½ tablespoons of the nut mixture into the bottom of the molds and top with ¼ cup of the rice mixture. Spread 2 heaping tablespoons of the cooled custard on the rice and refrigerate for 30 minutes, or until the custard is set. Sprinkle the top of each custard with about 1 teaspoon of sugar just prior to removing the mold.

ASSEMBLY Place one ring mold in the center of each plate and gently remove the molds. Caramelize the tops of the custards with a blowtorch until the sugar turns golden brown. Drizzle some of the Corn Sauce and Brown Butter–Corn Sauce around the plates and sprinkle with the shaved Brazil nuts.

Corn Sauce

Yield: approximately ¾ cup

½ cup freshly squeezed orange juice

1 tablespoon Simple Syrup (See Appendices)

3 tablespoons water

¾ cup corn

3 tablespoons heavy cream

METHOD Combine the orange juice, Simple Syrup, and water in a small pan. Add the corn and simmer until completely cooked and the juice is reduced by half. Purée the corn, cooking liquid, and cream for 1 minute, or until smooth. Strain through a fine-mesh sieve. Warm before serving, adding a small amount of orange juice if the sauce is too thick.

Brown Butter–Corn Sauce

Yield: approximately ½ cup

¼ cup unsalted butter

½ cup corn

2 tablespoons sugar

METHOD Brown the butter until it is very dark brown and has a nutty aroma. Add the corn and sugar and continue to cook for 5 minutes, or until the corn is cooked.

Date Tart with Pumpkin Custard and Pumpkin Seed Praline

This date tart is so dense and luscious that a sliver seems indulgent. Although the pumpkin and date flavors are both sweet, they blend perfectly. The flaky pastry and crunchy Pumpkin Seed Praline provide a textural counterpoint to the smooth, satiny date and pumpkin custard elements. This dessert works quite nicely either warm or at room temperature. For an even richer dessert, add a scoop of ice cream on the side.

Serves 6 to 8

Cream Cheese Dough (see Appendices)

1 cup cooked pumpkin, mashed

1 cup milk

1 egg

2 egg yolks

1/4 cup sugar

1 tablespoon orange zest

1/2 teaspoon ground cinnamon

1/4 teaspoon ground nutmeg

1/4 teaspoon ground mace

2 cups pitted dates, cut in half lengthwise

1 1/2 cups medium-diced raw pumpkin

1 1/2 cups water

1 cup freshly squeezed orange juice

2 cinnamon sticks

Pumpkin Seed Praline, made with whole seeds (see Appendices)

METHOD To prepare the crust: Roll out the Cream Cheese Dough to 1/8 inch thick. Place in a 9- or 10-inch tart pan or tart mold and refrigerate for 30 minutes. Trim the crust, leaving a 1/2-inch overhang. Fold the dough over and pinch, forming a vertical finished edge that extends 1/4 inch above the rim. Prick the bottom of the crust with a fork. Cover the bottom and sides of the crust with parchment, place dried beans or pie crust weights in the crust to prevent it from bubbling, and bake at 350 degrees for 15 to 20 minutes, or until lightly golden. Remove the parchment and beans and return the crust to the oven for 3 to 4 minutes, or until it is lightly browned throughout. (If there are any splits in the dough, repair them with the trimmed-off dough.)

To make the tart: Purée the cooked pumpkin with the milk. Add the egg, egg yolks, sugar, orange zest, cinnamon, nutmeg, and mace and stir until combined. Strain through a fine-mesh sieve and pour into the tart crust (it should fill the tart one-half to two-thirds full). Arrange the dates in a single layer on top of the custard and bake at 325 degrees for 30 to 40 minutes, or until set.

To make the sauce: Simmer the raw pumpkin, water, orange juice, and cinnamon sticks over medium heat for 30 minutes, or until the pumpkin can be easily mashed. Remove the cinnamon sticks and purée the pumpkin with the cooking liquid. Strain through a fine-mesh sieve. If the mixture seems too loose, continue cooking over medium heat for 15 minutes, or until it is a sauce consistency. If it is too thick, add water to thin it to the proper consistency.

ASSEMBLY Place a slice of the date tart in the center of each plate. Spoon some of the warm pumpkin sauce around the tart and sprinkle with the Pumpkin Seed Praline.

Brown Rice Pudding with Blue Hubbard Squash and Blackstrap Molasses Anglaise

~~~~~~

*This pudding may seem homespun compared with the others in this collection, but the flavors are
incredibly sophisticated. The brown rice retains its toothsome texture and lends a sublime nuttiness
to the overall flavor. Chunks of sweet, blue hubbard squash add a divine starchy character.
A final note of creamy, subdued sweetness is provided by a frothy molasses anglaise.
This dessert can be prepped in advance and served at either room temperature or hot out of the oven.
A scoop of ice cream can be added for more richness.*

Serves 10

1 1/2 cups medium-diced blue hubbard squash

1/4 cup firmly packed brown sugar

2 tablespoons unsalted butter, chopped

3/4 cup brown rice

1 3/4 cups water

1 cup milk

1 1/4 cups sugar

1 tablespoon orange zest

1 1/2 cups heavy cream

1/4 cup bourbon

3 eggs

1/8 teaspoon ground cinnamon

Dash of ground nutmeg

2 cups bread cubes

1 tablespoon freshly squeezed orange juice

1 cup small-diced blue hubbard squash

*Blackstrap Molasses Anglaise
(recipe follows)*

METHOD To roast the squash: Toss the medium-diced squash with the brown sugar and butter and roast at 350 degrees for 30 minutes, or until tender.

To cook the rice: Combine the rice, 1/2 cups of the water, the milk, 1/4 cup of the sugar, and the orange zest in a medium saucepan. Cover and cook over medium-low heat for 50 to 60 minutes, or until tender. Cool to room temperature and reserve 1/4 cup for garnish.

To make the pudding: Whisk together the cream, 2 tablespoons of the bourbon, the eggs, 1/2 cup of the sugar, the cinnamon, and nutmeg, pour over the bread cubes, and refrigerate for 30 minutes. Fold the rice and roasted squash into the bread cube mixture. Lightly oil the outsides of ten 2 1/2-inch-diameter by 1 1/2-inch-high ring molds. Wrap the bottom and two-thirds of the molds with plastic wrap. Place the molds upside down on a sheet pan and place in a 350-degree oven for about 10 seconds, or until the plastic shrinks onto the mold. Cool and invert on the sheet pan. Spoon the pudding into the molds, pressing down slightly to pack the molds. Bake in a water bath at 350 degrees for 35 to 40 minutes, or until the pudding is set.

To make the bourbon sauce: Combine the remaining 1/2 cup of sugar, 1/4 cup water, and 2 tablespoons bourbon with the orange juice and cook for about 5 minutes to reduce slightly. Add the small-diced squash and cook for 10 to 15 minutes, or until the squash is tender. Strain out the squash, reserving both the squash and the bourbon sauce.

METHOD Unmold a pudding in the center of each plate. Drizzle some of the bourbon sauce around the pudding. Spoon the Blackstrap Molasses Anglaise around the plate and sprinkle some of the squash and the reserved rice around the anglaise.

Blackstrap Molasses Anglaise

Yield: 1 cup

1 cup heavy cream

3 tablespoons sugar

1 tablespoon blackstrap molasses

1 egg yolk

METHOD Bring the cream to a boil. Whisk together the sugar, molasses, and egg yolk and slowly pour in some of the hot cream to temper the egg. Pour the egg mixture into the cream and cook for 2 to 3 minutes, or until the mixture coats the back of a spoon and steam rises from the top. Allow the mixture to cool slightly and then blend for 10 to 15 seconds to froth.

Custards

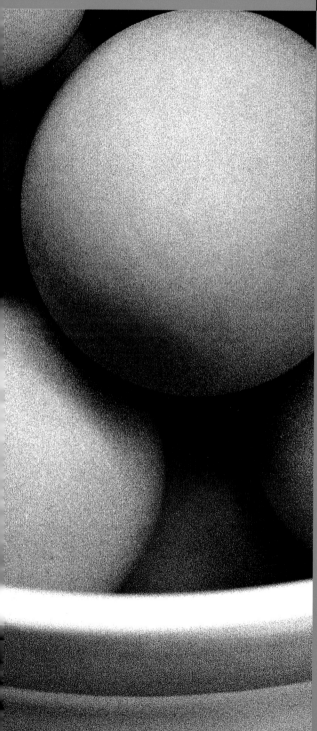

Sémillon is the classic match for custards. Its sweet fruitiness blends beautifully with the creamy custard, but still
provides enough acid to cut through some of the richness.

By far the greatest areas for this varietal are Sauternes
and Barsac, home of Chateau d'Yquem and many other
famous chateaux. *Boytritis cinerea*, or noble rot, is the magical, uncontrollable force that makes these sweet wines so
incredible. It is responsible for concentrating the sugar
and adding the honeyed, caramelized flavors. Sémillon also
expresses supporting flavors of vanilla and lemon cream,
which are very complementary to custard. Other styles of
late-harvest Sémillon, and even Sauvignon Blanc, emerging
from Washington State, New South Wales, and Napa Valley
can be equally great. Dolce, by Napa Valley's Far Niente, is
leading the pack; their older vintages are quite stunning
with custards and fruits alike.

Rosewater Crème Caramel with Primrose Sauce and Black Pepper Tuiles

Rosewater adds a majestic element to this simple crème caramel, and peppered tuile cookies add an elegantly cutting heat. Rose and black pepper seem meant for each other when sampled in a dessert like this. Each flavor complements the other while still shining on its own. Serve a warm fruit dessert after this and you'll be set.

Serves 8

1 cup heavy cream

1/2 cup milk

1 cup sugar

1 tablespoon orange zest

2 eggs

1 egg yolk

1 tablespoon rosewater

1/4 cup water

Primrose Sauce (recipe follows)

Black Pepper Tuiles (recipe follows)

METHOD To make the custard: Bring the cream, milk, 1/4 cup of the sugar, and the orange zest to a boil. Remove from the heat, cover, and steep for 30 minutes. Return the mixture to a boil. Whisk the eggs and egg yolk and slowly whisk in the hot cream mixture to temper the eggs. Mix thoroughly and strain through a fine-mesh sieve. Add the rosewater and mix well.

To make the caramel: Combine the remaining 3/4 cup sugar with the water in a small, heavy-bottomed sauté pan and cook over medium-high heat for 10 minutes, or until the mixture is deep golden brown and caramelized. Lightly oil eight 2- to 3-ounce rectangular molds. Pour 1 tablespoon of the caramelized sugar into the bottom of each mold, swirling to cover the entire bottom. Reserve any excess caramel. Ladle about 1/4 cup of the custard mixture into each mold and bake in a water bath at 325 degrees for 45 to 55 minutes, or until the custard is set. Refrigerate for at least 1 hour.

ASSEMBLY Remove the custard from the molds by gently loosening the sides with a knife. Lightly oil a spatula and, holding it over a bowl, invert each custard onto the spatula, catching any caramel in the bowl. Place a custard in the center of each plate. Drizzle the extra caramel and the Primrose Sauce around the plate. Insert pieces of the Black Pepper Tuiles into the center of each custard.

Primrose Sauce

Yield: 1/2 cup

1/2 cup Simple Syrup (see Appendices)

Petals of 3 primroses

1 blueberry or blackberry

METHOD Combine all of the ingredients in a blender and purée for 1 minute, or until smooth. Strain through a fine-mesh sieve.

Black Pepper Tuiles

Yield: 1/2 cup batter

1 1/2 tablespoons unsalted butter

Pulp of 1/4 vanilla bean

3 tablespoons flour

1 egg white

3/4 teaspoon black pepper

METHOD Melt the butter with the vanilla pulp and let cool slightly. Whisk the remaining ingredients into the butter mixture and pour into a squeeze bottle. Squeeze the batter out onto a Silpat-lined or nonstick sheet pan in the desired shapes and bake at 350 degrees for 3 to 5 minutes, or until light brown. Let cool and store in an airtight container at room temperature until needed.

Lavender and Almond Milk Flan
with Lavender Tuiles

This dessert is a light end to a luncheon or first course in a dessert progression. It's easy to prepare and can be made a day or so in advance for easy, last-minute assembly. The creamy custard and crispy tuile create a textural yin and yang, superbly showing off the regal flavor of the lavender. To give this dessert additional substance, a compote of peaches or berries can be added.

Serves 6

2 sheets gelatin

1 cup plus 2 tablespoons heavy cream

6 tablespoons milk

1/2 cup toasted almonds

1/4 cup sugar

2 tablespoons plus 1 1/2 teaspoons fresh lavender

1/2 cup Simple Syrup (see Appendices)

Lavender Tuiles (recipe follows)

METHOD To make the flan: Soak the gelatin in enough water to cover until it is softened. Bring the cream, milk, almonds, sugar, and 1½ teaspoons of the lavender to a boil. Remove from the heat, cover, and steep for 30 minutes. Add the gelatin, pour into 6 lightly oiled 3-ounce timbale molds, and refrigerate for 1 hour, or until firm.

To make the lavender sauce: Bring the Simple Syrup and 1 tablespoon of the lavender to a boil. Cover, and steep for 30 minutes. Pour into a blender, add the remaining 1 tablespoon lavender, and purée for 1 minute, or until smooth. Strain through a fine-mesh sieve and refrigerate.

ASSEMBLY Unmold a flan in the center of each plate. Place a Lavender Tuile around the flan and drizzle with the lavender sauce around both.

Lavender Tuiles

Yield: 8 to 12 tuiles

1/4 cup plus 1 1/2 teaspoons sugar

1 egg white

3 tablespoons unsalted butter, melted and cooled

1/4 cup plus 1 1/2 teaspoons flour

1 tablespoon fresh lavender

METHOD Whisk the sugar and egg white until soft peaks form. Fold in the melted butter and flour and refrigerate. Make a template by cutting the desired shape out of heavy plastic or cardboard. Place the template on a Silpat-lined or nonstick sheet pan and spread the batter onto the template, or spread the batter with a small offset spatula into a half-circle with a base about 5 inches long. Sprinkle each tuile with lavender petals. Repeat until all of the batter is used. Bake at 350 degrees for 5 to 7 minutes, or until lightly golden brown. Remove from the oven and immediately wrap the warm tuiles around a rolling pin or round mold to shape. Remove the tuiles from the mold while still slightly warm. If the tuiles harden before they are shaped, return them to the oven to soften.

Hoja Santa Crème Brûlée with Cactus Pear Sauce and White Honey–Tropical Fruit Compote

~~~~~~

This dish appears to be complicated, but it is actually fairly simple and certainly a showstopper. The anise-flavored hoja santa leaves can be tricky to find, but you can substitute rosemary or omit it altogether. The custard and the tuiles can both be made in advance. The fruit mixture can be served warm or cold, and once the custard is caramelized, the ingredients are easy to layer.

Serves 10

2 cups heavy cream

2 tablespoons chopped orange zest

1/2 hoja santa leaf, torn into pieces

5 egg yolks

1/4 cup plus 3 tablespoons sugar

2 cactus pears

5 tablespoons Simple Syrup (see Appendices)

1/4 cup freshly squeezed orange juice

1 sapote, cut into small dice (about 1/2 cup)

1 small papaya, cut into small rectangles (about 3/4 cup)

1 persimmon, cut into small wedges (about 1/2 cup)

1 mango, cut into small dice (about 3/4 cup)

2 tablespoons white honey

Macadamia Nut Tuiles (recipe follows)

Candied Hoja Santa (recipe follows)

METHOD To make the crème brûlée: Lightly oil the outsides of ten 2½-inch-diameter by 1½-inch-high ring molds. Wrap the bottom and lower two-thirds of the mold with plastic wrap. Place the molds upside down on a sheet pan and bake in a 350-degree oven for about 10 seconds, or until the plastic shrinks onto the mold. Cool and invert on the sheet pan. Bring the cream, orange zest, and hoja santa to a boil. Remove the pan from heat, cover, and steep for 30 minutes. Return the cream to a boil. Whisk together the egg yolks and 1/4 cup of the sugar. Slowly pour some of the hot cream into the eggs to temper the yolks. Pour the egg mixture back into the cream, mix well, and stir over low heat for 2 to 3 minutes to thicken slightly. Strain through a fine-mesh sieve and pour about 1/4 cup of the mixture into each ring mold. Bake in a water bath at 325 degrees for 20 to 25 minutes, or until the custard is set. Drain the water and refrigerate the custards.

To make the cactus pear sauce: Cut the cactus pears in half. Hold the pears in a towel to protect your hands from the small needles and scoop out the pulp. Combine the cactus pear pulp, Simple Syrup, and orange juice in a blender and purée for 1 minute, or until smooth. Strain through a fine-mesh sieve.

To prepare the compote: Cook the sapote, papaya, persimmon, and mango with the white honey until warm.

ASSEMBLY Place a Macadamia Nut Tuile in the center of each plate and top with a 2½-inch-diameter ring mold. Spoon about 1/4 cup of the warm fruit into the mold, reserving the honey sauce, and pack tightly. Remove the mold and top with another tuile. Sprinkle each custard with about 1 teaspoon of sugar and unmold the custards onto the tuiles. Caramelize the custards with a blowtorch for 10 seconds, or until light golden brown. Sprinkle the Candied Hoja Santa on top of the custards. Spoon some of the cactus pear sauce and honey sauce around each plate.

Macadamia Nut Tuiles

Yield: 20 to 24 tuiles

2 tablespoons unsalted butter

Pulp of 1/4 vanilla bean

1 egg white

3 tablespoons sugar

3 tablespoons flour

2 tablespoons toasted, ground macadamia nuts

METHOD Melt the butter with the vanilla pulp and remove from the heat to cool. Whisk the egg white until frothy, then slowly add the sugar and whip to soft peaks. Fold the butter mixture into the egg whites and mix well. Add the flour and stir until combined. Refrigerate for 30 minutes. Drop a generous 1/2 teaspoon of batter onto a Silpat-lined or nonstick sheet pan and, using a small offset spatula, spread it into a 2½ to 3-inch circle. Repeat until there are at least 20 tuiles. Sprinkle the tuiles with the ground macadamia nuts and bake at 350 degrees for 3 to 4 minutes, or until golden brown. Using a 2½-inch ring mold, cut each tuile to fit the mold exactly. Remove the tuiles from the pan while warm and place on the counter to cool. Store in an airtight container at room temperature until needed.

Candied Hoja Santa

Yield: approximately 1/4 cup

1 large hoja santa leaf, stem removed

2 tablespoons sugar

1 tablespoon water

1 drop of lemon juice

METHOD Finely chop the hoja santa. Cook the sugar, water, and lemon juice in a small, heavy-bottomed sauté pan for 5 minutes, or until light blond in color. Add the hoja santa, cook for 10 seconds, and pour onto a nonstick sheet pan. Let cool and then chop into small pieces.

Maple-Chestnut Custard Napoleon with Poached Pears and Pepper-Orange Sauce

All of the components in this dish can be prepped well in advance and then the dish can be assembled at the last moment—perfect for a special dinner party. Napoleons like this one are so easy to assemble and are so versatile that you can really have fun experimenting with different types of fruits and custards. The crispy filo provides an essential crunch that helps showcase the tremendous flavors of the dish, and the layered presentation allows for elegance and whimsy, simultaneously. In these napoleons, the flavor of the pears, maple syrup, chestnuts, and pecans blend seamlessly to create a dessert that foretells of the cold winter nights to come.

Serves 8

1/2 cup Sauternes

Pulp and pod of 1 vanilla bean

2 cinnamon sticks

1/2 cup water

1/2 cup freshly squeezed orange juice

1/3 cup granulated sugar

6 pears

1/4 teaspoon black pepper

6 sheets filo dough

1/2 cup unsalted butter, melted

Confectioners' sugar for dusting

Maple-Chestnut Custard (recipe follows)

1/2 cup Pecan Praline, chopped (see Appendices)

Pepper-Orange Sauce (recipe follows)

METHOD To prepare the pears: Bring the Sauternes, vanilla pulp and pod, cinnamon sticks, water, orange juice, and granulated sugar to a boil. Peel the pears and place them in the pan. Cover the pan with parchment paper and simmer for 20 to 30 minutes, or until the pears are tender and can be pierced easily with a knife blade. Let the pears cool in the liquid and then cut the pears crosswise into thirty-two 1/4-inch-thick slices. Cut out a small circle from the center of each slice and remove the core. Cut each slice with a round cutter to make them a uniform size. Dice the pear scraps, toss with the black pepper in a small bowl, and reserve for garnish.

To make the filo circles: Lay out a sheet of filo, brush with about 1 tablespoon of the melted butter and sprinkle lightly with confectioners' sugar. Cover with another sheet of filo, brush with another tablespoon of butter, lightly sprinkle with confectioners' sugar, cover with a final sheet of filo, and brush lightly with the butter. Repeat the process for a second stack with the remaining 3 sheets of filo. Using a ring cutter, cut 16 circles 1/4 inch larger than the pear slices out of both sets of filo dough. Place the circles on a parchment-lined sheet pan, cover with a sheet of parchment, and top with another sheet pan. Weight the sheet pan down with a brick or other heavy, ovenproof object. Bake at 375 degrees for 8 to 10 minutes, or until lightly browned.

ASSEMBLY Place a filo circle in the center of each plate. Top with a pear slice, a spoonful of Maple-Chestnut Custard, and a sprinkling of Pecan Praline. Repeat this process three more times for a total of 4 layers. Sprinkle some of the diced pears and Pecan Praline around the plate. Drizzle 2 tablespoons of Pepper-Orange Sauce around each plate.

Maple-Chestnut Custard

Yield: 4 cups

2/3 cup pure maple syrup
3/4 cup chestnuts, roasted, peeled, and chopped
2 cups heavy cream
3 egg yolks
1 egg
1/4 cup freshly squeezed orange juice

METHOD Simmer the maple syrup and chestnuts for 30 minutes, or until the chestnuts are cooked and the liquid is slightly reduced. Purée all the ingredients for 2 minutes, or until smooth. Strain through a fine-mesh sieve and pour into a 9 by 13-inch pan (the custard should be about 1/2 inch deep). Bake in a water bath at 350 degrees for 20 to 25 minutes, or until set. Remove from the water bath and refrigerate for at least 1 hour before serving.

Pepper-Orange Sauce

Yield: 1 cup

1 large pear, peeled, cored, and chopped
1/4 cup pure maple syrup
1/2 cup freshly squeezed orange juice
1/2 teaspoon black pepper

METHOD Cook the pear in the maple syrup and orange juice until tender. Purée the mixture for 2 minutes, or until smooth. Strain through a fine-mesh sieve and stir in the pepper.

Pecan Custard with Butternut Squash Chips and Pecan Meringue

Although this custard is slightly denser than a standard flan, it has a wonderful delicacy that showcases the flavor of the pecans. An airy pecan meringue and a slice of poached apple act as a base for the custard, providing both crunchy texture and fruity meatiness. Oven-dried butternut squash pieces provide a further textural note, and a barely astringent orange sauce cuts all of the elements, helping to perfectly balance all of the flavors. The harmony of these subdued flavors evokes fall.

Serves 6

1 butternut squash

5 tablespoons unsalted butter

2 tablespoons brown sugar

1 cup water

1 1/2 cups plus 2 1/2 tablespoons sugar

1/4 cup pecan halves, toasted

2 eggs

2 egg yolks

1 1/2 cups heavy cream

1/2 cup milk

1/8 teaspoon ground cinnamon

1/8 teaspoon ground nutmeg

2 Fuji apples, cored

2/3 cup freshly squeezed orange juice

1 cinnamon stick

1 tablespoon egg white

1/4 teaspoon ground cinnamon

1/8 teaspoon ground cayenne pepper

1/4 cup pecan halves, cut lengthwise into thirds

Pecan Meringue (recipe follows)

METHOD To prepare the squash: Cut the neck from the squash and reserve for the squash chips. Cut the remaining squash in quarters and place on a sheet pan. Dot the flesh with 2 tablespoons of the butter and sprinkle with the brown sugar. Fill the pan with 1/4 inch of water and bake at 350 degrees for 1 hour, or until soft.

To make the squash chips: Peel the reserved squash and then cut it into thin slices with a vegetable peeler. Bring the water and 1/2 cup of the sugar to a boil, add the squash strips, and cook over medium heat for 5 minutes. Remove from the water, place on a Silpat-lined or nonstick sheet pan, and bake at 225 degrees for 1 hour, or until dry and crispy. Carefully remove from the sheet pan to cool.

To make the custard: Purée 1 cup of squash, 1/4 cup of the sugar, the toasted pecans, eggs, egg yolks, the cream, milk, cinnamon, and nutmeg in a blender for 2 minutes, or until smooth. Strain through a fine-mesh sieve and pour in an 8 by 8-inch oiled and plastic wrap–lined pan. Bake in a water bath at 350 degrees for 25 to 35 minutes, or until set. Refrigerate to chill completely, turn out onto a sheet pan, and cut into 2 1/2-inch circles. Sprinkle each custard round with 1 teaspoon of sugar and caramelize with a blowtorch. Before the caramel hardens, place a few squash chips upright in the center of the custard.

To make the apples: Cut the top and bottom from each apple and slice crosswise into 3 pieces. If the apple is larger than 3 1/2 inches, use a cutter to reduce it to that size. Cook the remaining 3 tablespoons butter until the butter is brown and has a nutty aroma. Press the apple slices in 1/2 cup of the sugar to coat. Add the apples to the butter and cook for 3 to 4 minutes, or until caramelized and golden brown. Turn the slices over and continue to cook for 3 to 4 minutes.

To make the sauce: Bring 1 cup of the squash, the orange juice, 1/4 cup of the sugar and the cinnamon stick to a boil. Strain through a fine-mesh sieve, pressing on the squash to remove as much liquid as possible. If the sauce is too thin, return it to the pan and cook over medium heat until reduced to the desired consistency. If it is too thick, add a small amount of orange juice to thin it.

To make the candied pecans: Whisk together the egg whites, the remaining 1 1/2 teaspoons sugar, the ground cinnamon, and cayenne pepper until frothy. Toss the pecans in the mixture until completely coated. Place the pecans on a nonstick sheet pan and bake at 325 degrees for 5 to 7 minutes, or until browned.

ASSEMBLY Place an apple slice in the center of each plate and top with a Pecan Meringue. Place a custard circle on each meringue. Spoon the squash sauce around the plate and sprinkle with the candied pecans.

Pecan Meringue

Yield: 6 to 8 meringues

1/3 cup egg whites

1/4 cup sugar

2 tablespoons pecans, toasted and ground

METHOD Trace six to eight 3-inch circles on a parchment-lined sheet pan. In an electric mixer, whip the egg whites until they are frothy. Pour in the sugar and continue to beat until soft peaks form. Fold in the nuts, place the mixture in a pastry bag, and pipe onto the circles. Bake at 225 degrees for 2 hours, or until both the tops and the bottoms are dry.

Crispy Tapioca Pudding
with Elderberries and Mint Syrup

*This tapioca pudding tart is sensually satisfying, but also has an arresting tartness compliments
of the elderberries. This is a great make-ahead dessert. The tart shells and the Mint Syrup
can be made in the morning, and then you just heat the elderberries, add the tapioca to the shells,
and caramelize the tops of the tarts at the last minute. If elderberries are unavailable,
a compote of tropical fruits or even braised apples or pears could be substituted.*

Serves 6

Cream Cheese Dough (see Appendices)

2¼ cups milk

¼ cup freshly squeezed orange juice

1 cup sugar

Pulp of ½ vanilla bean

½ cup tapioca

2 tablespoons water

2 cups elderberries

Mint Syrup (see Appendices)

1 tablespoon julienned mint leaves

METHOD To make the tart shells: Place six 3-inch-diameter by ½-inch-high tart rings on a parchment-lined sheet pan. Roll out the Cream Cheese Dough to ⅛ inch thick, cut into six 4-inch circles, and press into the tart rings. Refrigerate for at least 30 minutes. Trim off the excess dough and prick the bottoms of the shells with a fork. Fill each tart ring with a piece of parchment paper and dried beans or pie crust weights. If the dough softens as you are working, return it to the refrigerator to firm up. Bake at 350 degrees for 15 to 20 minutes, or until the dough is set. Remove the parchment and weights and return the shells to the oven for 5 to 10 minutes, or until golden brown and fully cooked.

To make the tarts: Heat the milk, orange juice, 6 tablespoons of the sugar, and the vanilla until just warm. Add the tapioca and simmer, stirring frequently, for 20 to 25 minutes, or until the tapioca is cooked but still has a slightly firm center. Remove from the heat and cool. Spoon about 2 tablespoons of the filling into each tart shell, smoothing the mixture to reach the edges of the shell. Sprinkle each tart with 1 tablespoon of the sugar. Caramelize the sugar using a blowtorch for 10 seconds, or until golden brown.

To make the sauce: Cook the remaining ¼ cup sugar and the water in a small sauté pan over medium heat for 5 minutes, or until golden brown and caramelized. Remove from the heat, add the elderberries, and stir until coated. Return to the heat for about 2 minutes to warm the berries and release the juices.

ASSEMBLY Spoon the elderberries and juice around each plate. Place a tart in the center of each plate on top of the elderberries. Drizzle the Mint Syrup around the plates and sprinkle with the julienned mint.

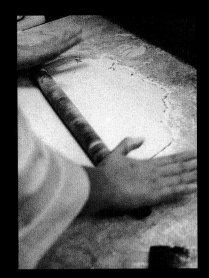

Your motive by working should be to set others, by your example, on the path of duty. – BHAGAVAD GITA

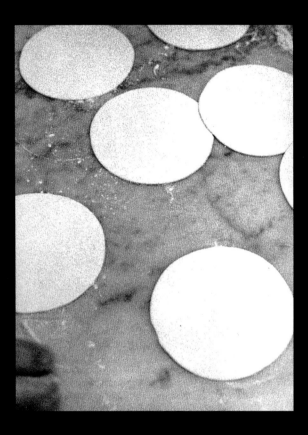

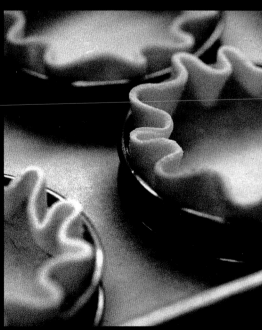

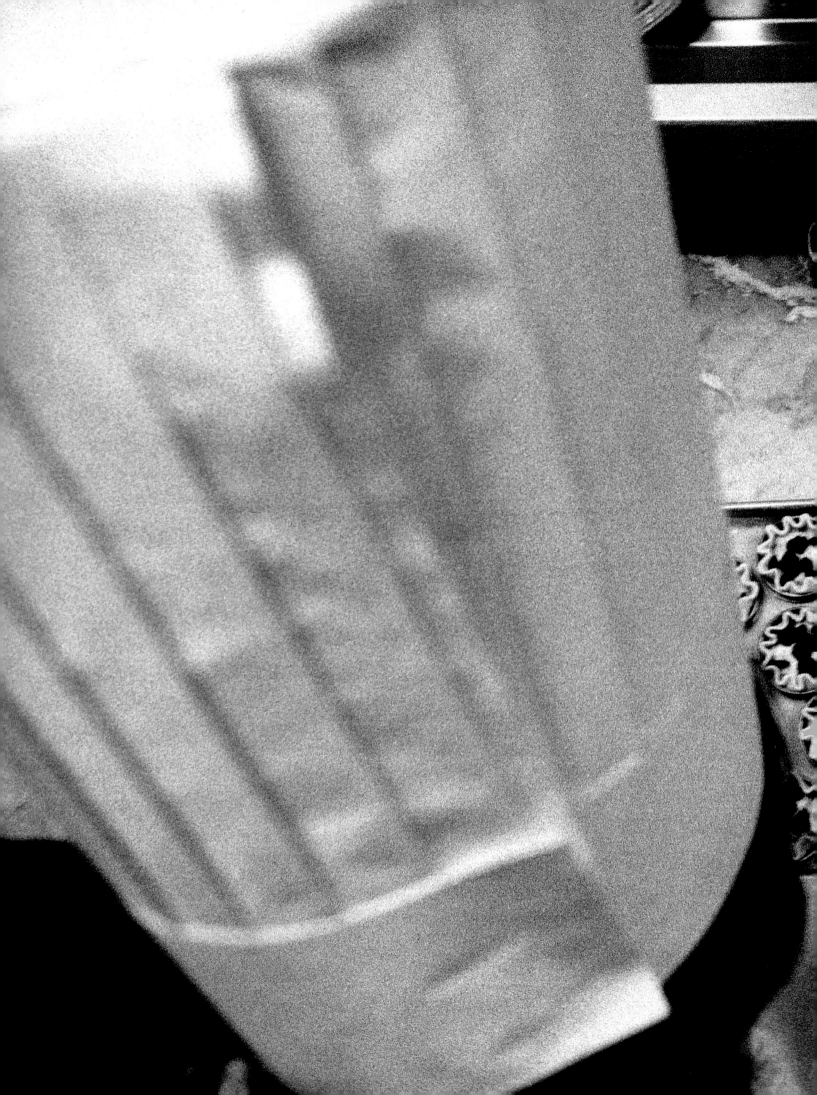

Concord Grape and Goat Cheese Cheesecake

*Cheesecake is always a favorite, but goat cheese and Concord grapes give this two-layered version
a special twist. Since this cheesecake is not overly sweet, the flavors of the goat cheese
and the Concord grapes are fully discernable. The two flavors are superbly compatible,
even complementary. The clean, fruity acid of the grapes perfectly cuts into the creamy, mustiness
of the cheese. Pieces of grape add a further cleansing note and a wonderful textural element.
This cheesecake can be made up to two days in advance and simply plated with the sauce
at the last minute. To lift this dish to another level, try crumbling a little goat cheese
on and around the cake and adding a couple of roasted hazelnuts to each plate.*

Serves 6

½ cup cold unsalted butter, cubed

¾ cup plus 2 tablespoons sugar

1 cup flour

Pinch of salt

3 tablespoons unsalted butter, melted

7 cups fresh Concord grapes

1 cup water

1 cup heavy cream

6 ounces goat cheese

6 ounces cream cheese

2 eggs

Pulp of 1 vanilla bean

*2 tablespoons Simple Syrup
(see Appendices)*

METHOD To make the crust: Cream the cubed butter and ¼ cup of the sugar until smooth. Add the flour and salt and mix until combined. Roll out the dough to ¼ inch thick, cover, and refrigerate for 1 hour. Place the chilled dough on a parchment-lined sheet pan and bake at 350 degrees for 10 to 12 minutes, or until golden. Let cool, then finely crumble into a bowl. Add the melted butter and 2 tablespoons of the sugar and mix well. Line a 6 by 6-inch pan with heavy-duty aluminum foil, extending the foil over the edges of the pan, and press the crust mixture into the bottom of the pan.

To make the grape juice: Simmer 6 cups of the grapes and the water for 30 minutes, or until the grapes are easily crushed. Strain through a fine-mesh sieve, pressing on the solids to remove as much liquid as possible. Return the juice to the heat and cook for 20 minutes, or until reduced to 1 cup.

To make the cheesecake: Bring the cream and the remaining ½ cup of sugar to a boil. Simmer for 15 to 20 minutes, or until reduced to ¾ cup. Remove from the heat and let cool slightly. Cream the goat cheese and cream cheese, add the sweetened cream and eggs, and mix until smooth. Place half of the mixture in a separate bowl and mix in the vanilla pulp. Add ½ cup of the grape juice to the remaining batter, spread the batter into the pan, and refrigerate for 30 minutes to firm slightly. Spread the vanilla batter on top of the chilled grape batter and bake in a water bath at 325 degrees for 45 minutes, or until set. Refrigerate overnight.

For the garnish: Peel the skins from the remaining 1 cup grapes, cut the grapes in half, remove the seeds, and toss with the Simple Syrup.

ASSEMBLY Lift the cheesecake out of the pan and cut into 2 by 3-inch pieces. Place a piece of cheesecake in the center of each plate and spoon the reserved grape juice over the cheesecake and around the plates. Sprinkle some of the halved grapes on the cheesecake and around the plates.

Peanut Butter Pudding with Bananas and Brown Butter Sauce

This lavish combination of peanut butter and bananas becomes even more sinful with the addition of the rich, nutty, brown butter sauce. Peanut praline and a chocolate crust heighten the decadence. A ribbony piece of banana "leather" provides a marvelous, chewy texture, as it reiterates the banana flavor. This dish is perfect for anyone who loves gooey, creamy, luscious desserts, and it can be made in advance for easy, last-minute assembly.

Serves 6

¹/₂ cup unsalted butter

¹/₄ cup confectioners' sugar

¹/₄ cup unsweetened cocoa

¹/₄ cup flour

¹/₄ cup finely chopped roasted peanuts

1 cup plus 2 tablespoons heavy cream

1 egg

3 egg yolks

³/₄ cup granulated sugar

¹/₄ cup high-quality, smooth peanut butter

¹/₄ cup water

8 Cuban bananas, peeled and quartered, lengthwise

Pulp and pod of 1 vanilla bean

2 whole ripe bananas, peeled

1 egg white

¹/₄ cup Peanut Praline, ground (see Appendices)

METHOD To make the crust: Cream ¹/₄ cup of the butter and the confectioners' sugar. Add the cocoa, flour, and peanuts, and mix in an electric mixer fitted with the paddle attachment until the dough comes together. Divide the dough among six 2¹/₂-inch-diameter ring molds on a parchment-lined sheet pan and pat it into the bottom of the molds. Refrigerate the crusts for 30 minutes, or until chilled and then bake at 350 degrees for 10 minutes. Remove the ring molds while the crusts are still hot.

To make the custard: Prepare an ice water bath. Bring 1 cup of the cream to a boil. Whisk together the egg, egg yolks, and ¹/₄ cup of the sugar in a small bowl. Slowly pour in some of the hot cream to temper the eggs. Pour the eggs into the cream mixture and cook over low heat for 2 to 3 minutes, or until the mixture coats the back of a spoon and steam rises from the top. Whisk in the peanut butter. Strain through a fine-mesh sieve and cool over the ice water bath, stirring occasionally, until chilled.

Lightly oil the outsides of six 2¹/₂-inch-diameter by 1¹/₂-inch-high ring molds. Wrap the lower two-thirds of the molds with plastic wrap. Place the molds upside down on a sheet pan and place in a 350-degree oven for about 10 seconds, or until the plastic shrinks onto the mold. Let cool, then invert the molds on the sheet pan. Pour the custard into the molds and bake in a water bath at 350 degrees for 25 to 30 minutes, or until set. Remove from the oven, carefully drain the water, let cool, and refrigerate.

To make the bananas: Cook the remaining ¹/₂ cup sugar and the water in a small, heavy-bottomed sauté pan over medium heat for 5 minutes, or until light golden brown. Place the quartered bananas in the pan and remove from the heat. Let the bananas sit in the caramel sauce for 15 seconds on each side, turning them carefully to avoid breakage. Remove the bananas from the pan, reserving the juices.

To make the brown butter sauce: Brown the remaining ¹/₄ cup of butter with the vanilla pulp until the butter is dark brown and has a nutty aroma. Add the browned butter and the remaining 2 tablespoons of cream to the banana pan juices and stir until combined. If the sauce is too thick, stir in a small amount of hot water.

To make the banana chips: Purée the whole bananas and egg white until smooth. Spread the batter onto a Silpat-lined or nonstick sheet pan in a very thin layer. Bake at 225 degrees for 45 to 60 minutes, or until the batter has set enough to cut. Cut into 1¹/₂ by 6-inch strips. Lift the strips from the pan to loosen, then return the pan to the oven to continue baking for 10 to 15 minutes, or until the strips are strong enough to shape. Remove the strips and bend them into the desired shapes. If they do not become crisp, return them to the oven to cook for a few more minutes.

ASSEMBLY Arrange 5 of the banana quarters side by side in the center of each plate. Hold the custard over the crust and gently push the edges of the mold to release the custard. Sprinkle the custards with some of the ground Peanut Praline and place on the bananas. Top with a banana chip and drizzle the brown butter sauce around the plate.

Nuts

Nuts provide some of the earthiest, richest flavors in desserts, and wines that reinforce these flavors are the most suitable mates for them. Whether they are dry or sweet, sherries have always enjoyed a wonderful nuttiness.  The decadently sweet style of a Moscatel or a Pedro Ximénex will be brilliant with desserts that contain nuts, toffee, or brittle. Another incredible combination would be an old Barsac. The wines from the commune of Barsac are not as sweet as those from the other communes of Bomme, Fargues, Preignac, or Sauternes. When aged for twenty years or so, these wines take on elegant, nutty flavors that are wonderful with hazelnuts and brittles. For moderately sweet desserts, a sweet, old Madeira, such as a Bual or Malmsey, will be a perfect match.

Cranberry and Walnut Tart
with Cranberry Ice Cream and
Cranberry and Caramel-Lime Sauces

This make-ahead dessert can be served either warm or at room temperature. The cranberries in this dessert have a wonderful sweet-tart flavor that is emphasized by the creamy yet austere ice cream. The caramel-lime and cranberry sauces deliver poised, adult flavors. The walnuts add a soothing meatiness. In all, it's a simple but profound weaving of earthy and poetic flavors and textures.

Serves 6

Pâte Sucrée (recipe follows)

5 tablespoons sugar

¼ cup firmly packed brown sugar

½ cup corn syrup

1 tablespoon plus 1 teaspoon unsalted butter

½ teaspoon pure vanilla extract

Pinch of salt

1 egg

1 egg yolk

¼ cup dried cranberries

2½ ounces walnut pieces, toasted

Cranberry Ice Cream (recipe follows)

Cranberry Sauce (recipe follows)

Caramel-Lime Sauce (recipe follows)

METHOD To make the tart shells: Roll out the Pâte Sucrée to 1/16 inch thick. Place six 3-inch-diameter by ½-inch-high tart rings on a parchment-lined sheet pan. Cut six 4-inch circles from the dough and press them into the rings. Refrigerate until firm, then trim the excess dough.

To make the tarts: Combine the sugar, brown sugar, and corn syrup. Brown the butter until it is smoky and has a nutty aroma. Remove from the heat, immediately add the butter to the sugar mixture, and mix well. Add the vanilla and salt and mix thoroughly. Allow the mixture to cool, then add the egg and egg yolk. Evenly distribute the cranberries and walnuts among the tart rings. Fill the tarts one-third to halfway full with the sugar mixture (about 2 tablespoons per tart). Bake at 350 degrees for 15 to 20 minutes, or until the dough is golden brown and the filling is bubbly.

ASSEMBLY Place a cranberry tart in the center of each plate and top with a quenelle of Cranberry Ice Cream. Drizzle about 1 tablespoon each of Cranberry Sauce and Caramel-Lime Sauce around the plates.

Pâte Sucrée

Yield: 6 individual tarts

1 cup flour

⅓ cup cold unsalted butter

⅓ cup sugar

Pinch of salt

1 egg yolk

1 tablespoon plus 1 teaspoon heavy cream

METHOD Using an electric mixer on low speed, combine the flour, butter, sugar, and salt until it forms pebble-size balls. Combine the egg yolk and cream, add it to the flour, and mix just until the dough comes together. Remove the dough from the mixer, pat into a disc, and cover in plastic wrap. Refrigerate to chill thoroughly before rolling.

Cranberry Ice Cream

Yield: approximately 3 cups

2 cups fresh cranberries

2 cups heavy cream

1 tablespoon orange zest

4 egg yolks

½ cup sugar

METHOD Cook the cranberries, cream, and orange zest over medium heat, stirring occasionally, for 10 minutes, or until the cranberries completely break down. Crush the cranberries against the side of the pan with the back of the spoon. Whisk together the egg yolks and sugar and slowly pour in some of the hot cream to temper the eggs. Pour the eggs into the cream mixture and cook over low heat, stirring continuously, for 2 to 3 minutes, or until it coats the back of a spoon and steam rises from the top. Strain through a fine-mesh sieve, pressing on the solids to remove as much liquid as possible. Cool over an ice water bath, stirring occasionally, until chilled. Freeze in an ice cream machine and keep frozen until ready to serve.

Cranberry Sauce

Yield: ⅓ cup

½ cup fresh cranberries

2 tablespoons freshly squeezed orange juice

2 tablespoons Simple Syrup (see Appendices)

METHOD Purée all of the ingredients until smooth. Pour the mixture through a strainer, pressing on the cranberries to allow some of the pulp to pass through. Refrigerate until ready to use.

Caramel-Lime Sauce

Yield: ½ cup

½ cup sugar

¼ cup water

¼ cup freshly squeezed lime juice, plus additional as necessary

METHOD Cook the sugar and water in a small, heavy-bottomed sauté pan over medium-high heat for 5 minutes, or until deep golden brown and caramelized. Remove from the heat, add the lime juice, and mix thoroughly. Allow the sauce to cool before serving. If the sauce is too thick when it cools, thin with additional lime juice.

In the long run you hit only what you aim at. Therefore, though you shou

*The simple flavors of this dish will really capture the attention of your guests.
The sabayon is so light it literally disappears as it hits your tongue, and the chestnuts,
while earthy, demonstrate their true by majestic of flavor and texture. When serving the wontons
hot from the fryer, you will experience an extraordinary temperature contrast, as well.
This is definitely a dessert to linger over with a great old Cognac or an even older Madeira.*

erves 6

¹/₂ cups chestnuts, roasted

cups water

¹/₄ cups Simple Syrup (see Appendices)

¼ cup freshly squeezed lemon juice

tablespoons crème fraîche

¼ cup freshly squeezed orange juice

4 (3-inch) round wonton skins

egg, beaten

Oil for frying

Confectioners' sugar, for dusting

Vanilla-Mascarpone Sabayon
(recipe follows)

METHOD To prepare the chestnuts: Carefully peel the chestnuts, keeping at least 12 whole for the wontons. Simmer the chestnuts in the water for 10 minutes. Remove 1 cup of chestnut pieces and reserve for the filling. Add 1 cup of the Simple Syrup and the lemon juice to the pan and simmer for 20 minutes. Remove the chestnuts from the liquid and cool. Set aside 12 whole chestnuts and slice the remaining nuts into ⅛-inch-thick slices.

To make the filling: Purée the reserved chestnut pieces, the remaining ¼ cup of the Simple Syrup, the crème fraîche, and orange juice for 2 minutes, or until smooth.

To assemble the wontons: Lay out 12 wonton skins on the work surface. Place 1 tablespoon of the chestnut purée in the center of each wonton and top with a whole chestnut. Brush the remaining wonton skins with egg and center one wonton skin, egg-wash side facing down, over each chestnut. Lift the wonton and pinch the edges together to seal them, being careful not to trap air inside. Pour 3 inches of oil into a pot and heat to 325 degrees. Test the temperature by putting in a piece of wonton skin: if it browns too quickly, reduce the heat to allow the oil to cool down. Deep-fry the wontons for 3 to 4 minutes, or until golden brown, turning them over halfway through to ensure even browning. Transfer the wontons to a paper towel, let cool slightly, and dust both sides with confectioners' sugar. Cut each wonton in half.

ASSEMBLY Divide the Vanilla-Mascarpone Sabayon among 6 bowls. Arrange 4 wonton halves in each bowl and sprinkle with the chestnut slices.

Vanilla-Mascarpone Sabayon

Yield: 3 cups

5 egg yolks

½ cup Vanilla Simple Syrup
(see Appendices)

2 tablespoons orange zest

1 cup mascarpone

METHOD Prepare an ice water bath. Whisk the egg yolks, Simple Syrup, and orange zest in a metal bowl over barely simmering water until it triples in volume and reaches the ribbon stage. Strain through a fine-mesh sieve and cool over the ice water bath, stirring occasionally, until chilled. Whip the mascarpone with an electric mixer for 1 minute. Add the chilled sabayon and continue to whip for 1 more minute. Refrigerate until ready to use.

Macadamia Nut Chocolate Cake with Coconut Emulsion and Sugarcane Ice Cream

When you eat this dessert, you will no doubt find that it renders you speechless,
or that you don't really care to speak. Bittersweet chocolate, macadamia nuts, and coconut
are gloriously married, needing only a scoop of hauntingly simple Sugarcane Ice Cream for the
finish. The macadamia nut cakes can be baked in advance and served at room temperature,
but taking the extra effort to serve them right out of the oven is worth the trouble.
If you desire more intensity, substitute chocolate ice cream for the Sugarcane Ice Cream.

Serves 6

3 ounces toasted macadamia nuts

3/4 cup unsalted butter

1 cup sugar

4 eggs

1/2 cup unsweetened cocoa, sifted

1/2 cup flour

1/4 teaspoon baking powder

Vanilla Tuile Batter (see Appendices)

1 cup milk

1 tablespoon orange zest

1/2 cup toasted unsweetened coconut

Chocolate Sauce (see Appendices)

Sugarcane Ice Cream (recipe follows)

METHOD To make the cake: Finely grind half of the macadamia nuts and coarsely chop the remaining half. Cream the butter and sugar and add the eggs one at a time, mixing well after each addition. Add the cocoa, flour, and baking powder and stir until fully incorporated. Gently fold the ground nuts into the batter. Place six 2½-inch-diameter by 1½-inch-high buttered ring molds on a parchment-lined sheet pan. Fill the molds two-thirds full with the batter and sprinkle with the chopped macadamia nuts. Bake at 350 degrees for 15 to 20 minutes, or until a toothpick inserted in the center of the cakes comes out clean.

To make the tuiles: Spread the Vanilla Tuile Batter in a very thin layer on the back of a nonstick sheet pan. Bake at 325 degrees for 10 minutes, or until the batter has set enough to cut it with a knife or a pizza cutter. Cut at least six 1 by 6-inch strips. Return the pan to the oven for 3 to 4 more minutes, or until the strips are golden brown. Remove the pan from the oven and immediately form the strips into circles with a 1½-inch overlap where the ends meet. If the tuiles harden on the sheet pan, return them to the oven briefly to soften.

To make the coconut emulsion: Bring the milk, orange zest, and coconut to a boil. Remove from the heat, cover, and steep for 30 minutes. Purée the mixture until smooth and strain through a fine-mesh sieve. Warm just prior to serving and mix with a handheld blender until frothy.

ASSEMBLY Place a cake in the center of each plate. Encircle the cakes with a ring of Chocolate Sauce around the plate (a squeeze bottle works well for this). Spoon the coconut emulsion inside the ring of Chocolate Sauce. Place a small scoop of Sugarcane Ice Cream inside each tuile ring and set the tuiles on top of the cakes.

Sugarcane Ice Cream

Yield: 3 cups

2 cups heavy cream

1 8-ounce stalk sugarcane, peeled and diced (3/4 to 1 cup)

1 teaspoon lemon zest

4 egg yolks

1/4 cup sugar

METHOD Bring the cream, sugarcane, and lemon zest to a boil. Cover, remove from the heat, and steep for 30 minutes. Prepare an ice water bath. Return the cream to a boil. Whisk together the egg yolks and sugar and slowly pour in some of the hot cream to temper the eggs. Pour the eggs into the cream mixture and cook for 2 to 3 minutes, or until the mixture coats the back of a spoon and steam rises from the top. Purée until smooth and strain through a fine-mesh sieve. Cool over the ice water bath, stirring occasionally, until chilled. Freeze in an ice cream machine and keep frozen until ready to use.

Black Truffle Ice Cream with Organic Ennis Hazelnuts

Yes, black truffles can work in ice cream! This very heady preparation is enough to bring diners to their knees, as these lusty, earthy flavors utterly paralyze with sublime sensuality. Rich, sweet, earthy hazelnuts not only highlight the outrageous truffle flavor but also provide an essential textural component. Serve this as an early dessert course before a warm pear or apple tart and you will leave your guests with the memory of taste and flavor sensations they will talk about forever.

Serves 8 to 10

4 ounces toasted Ennis hazelnuts
1 large black truffle
2 tablespoons unsalted butter
3 tablespoons freshly squeezed orange juice
1/2 cup Simple Syrup (see Appendices)
1 tablespoon black truffle oil
Black Truffle Ice Cream (recipe follows)

METHOD To prepare the nuts: Rub the hazelnuts with a towel to remove any loosened skins. Cut the nuts in quarters. Pick out the nuts that don't cut evenly and shave them on a mandoline or grater.

To prepare the truffles: Slice the black truffles with a mandoline or cut them as thinly as possible with a sharp knife. Julienne the uneven ends and reserve. Bring the butter, orange juice, Simple Syrup, and truffle oil to a simmer. Add the black truffles just before serving.

ASSEMBLY Make 8 to 10 quenelles of Black Truffle Ice Cream. Trim one end of each quenelle flat, and set a quenelle upright in the center of each plate. Using a fork, remove the black truffle slices from the liquid and arrange them around the ice cream. Spoon the julienned truffles around the plate with some of the liquid. Arrange the hazelnut quarters on the black truffle slices and sprinkle the shaved hazelnuts over the ice cream and sliced truffles.

Black Truffle Ice Cream

Yield: approximately 2 to 3 cups

2 cups heavy cream
1 tablespoon orange zest
2 ounces black truffle, chopped
4 egg yolks
1/4 cup sugar

METHOD Bring the cream, orange zest, and half of the black truffle to a boil. Remove from the heat, cover, and steep for 30 minutes. Prepare an ice water bath. Return to a boil. Whisk together the egg yolks and sugar and slowly pour in some of the hot cream to temper the eggs. Pour the egg mixture into the cream and cook for 2 to 3 minutes, or until the mixture coats the back of a spoon and steam rises from the top. Cool over the ice water bath, stirring occasionally, until chilled. Purée the mixture until smooth and strain through a fine-mesh sieve. Add the remaining chopped black truffle to the mixture and freeze in an ice cream machine. Keep frozen until ready to use.

Thus to be independent of public opinion is the first formal condition of achieving anything great

G.W.F. Hegel

Pecan Pie with Blackstrap Molasses
and Sweet Curry Crust

*This pecan pie is given an exotic twist by incorporating curry in the pastry,
demonstrating how curry can work in sweet as well as savory preparations. In this dish,
the pie is served with lightly whipped cream and a dusting of pulverized curried pecans.
Vanilla ice cream could substitute nicely for the whipped cream.*

Serves 8

4 ounces cream cheese, cut into chunks

½ cup unsalted butter plus 2 tablespoons, cut into chunks

1 cup flour

1½ teaspoons sweet curry powder

1½ teaspoons orange zest, chopped

8 ounces pecans, lightly toasted

5 tablespoons firmly packed brown sugar

7 tablespoons sugar

¼ cup bourbon

2 tablespoons blackstrap molasses

½ cup plus 2 tablespoons corn syrup

Pulp and pod of 1 vanilla bean

3 egg yolks

½ cup heavy cream

Caramel Sauce (recipe follows)

Curried Pecans (recipe follows)

METHOD To make the crust: Combine the cream cheese, ½ cup of the butter, the flour, curry powder, and orange zest in a large mixing bowl. Using an electric mixer fitted with the paddle attachment, mix until just combined. Form the dough into a disc, cover in plastic wrap, and refrigerate for at least 1 hour. Roll out the dough to ⅛ inch thick and place it into a 10-inch tart ring. Trim the dough ½ inch above the ring. Fold the dough back just to the rim of the ring and gently pinch it to create an edge that extends ¼ inch above the ring. Refrigerate for 30 minutes. Prick the bottom of the crust with a fork and place a piece of parchment in the crust. Fill with dried beans or other piecrust weights and bake at 350 degrees for 15 minutes, or until set and lightly browned. Remove the parchment and weights and return the crust to the oven for an additional 3 to 4 minutes, or until the crust is golden brown.

To make the filling: Spread the pecans evenly in the bottom of the crust. Combine the brown sugar, 3 tablespoons of the sugar, the bourbon, molasses, and corn syrup. Brown the remaining 2 tablespoons butter with the vanilla pulp and bean until the butter is dark brown and has a nutty aroma. Remove the vanilla bean, pour the brown butter over the sugar mixture, and mix well. Add the egg yolks and stir until completely incorporated. Pour the filling over the pecans and bake the pie at 350 degrees for 20 minutes, or until set. Cool and cut into 8 pieces.

To make the cream: Whip the cream with the remaining 4 tablespoons sugar until soft peaks form.

ASSEMBLY Place a slice of pie in the center of each plate and top with a spoonful of the whipped cream. Drizzle the Caramel Sauce around the plate and sprinkle the slivered and ground Curried Pecans on top of the pie and around the plate.

Caramel Sauce

Yield: approximately 1½ cups

1 cup sugar

¼ cup water

½ cup freshly squeezed orange juice, strained and warmed

METHOD Cook the sugar and water in a heavy-bottomed sauté pan over medium heat for 10 minutes, or until medium brown and caramelized. Turn off the heat and slowly add the orange juice. Bring to a boil, stirring to dissolve any hardened sugar. Remove from the heat and let cool to room temperature.

Curried Pecans

Yield: 1 cup

¼ cup sugar

2 tablespoons water

¾ cup pecan halves, toasted

1 tablespoon unsalted butter

½ teaspoon sweet curry powder

½ teaspoon paprika

⅛ teaspoon ground cayenne pepper

⅛ teaspoon pepper

METHOD Cook the sugar and water in a small, heavy-bottomed sauté pan over medium heat for 5 minutes, or until light brown and caramelized. Reduce the heat, add the nuts, and stir until completely coated. Add the butter, curry powder, paprika, cayenne, and pepper and stir until the spices are evenly distributed. Pour onto a Silpat-lined or nonstick sheet pan, separating the nuts, and let cool. Set aside 3 tablespoons for grinding and cut the remaining nuts lengthwise into thirds. Grind 3 tablespoons of Curried Pecans in a blender.

Spices

Spice is not usually the defining element for the flavors in these recipes, but will lead you in the direction of spicier wines. Molasses and coffee are better with wines that have more extended wood-aging and tend to take on more spice notes. Late Bottled Vintage Port is a spicier style than most vintage ports because it is wood-aged slightly longer and has a greater concentration of fruit. Vintages of Taylor Fladgate from the late eighties and early nineties still have an intense fruitiness and array of earthy flavors that will harmonize with desserts that have a coffee element. Ten- and twenty-year Tawny Ports become even more mellow and spicy than Late Bottled Vintage Ports, yet retain much of their youthful fruit flavors and complement the more delicate spice and carrot cakes.

Ginger-Molasses Spice Cake
with Mascarpone Cream and
Clear Lady Apple Chips

*This fragrant spice cake is perfect as a light ending to a substantial meal
or as an early course in a dessert progression. The cake can even be served
as part of a breakfast menu because it is not very sweet. This is a great make-ahead
preparation; the cake does not suffer in any way from being baked the day before.*

Serves 9

½ cup finely chopped peeled ginger

¼ cup freshly squeezed orange juice

½ cup milk (approximately)

2 tablespoons brandy

1½ teaspoons rice wine vinegar

½ cup unsalted butter

2⅓ cups plus 2 tablespoons granulated sugar

2 eggs

¾ cup light molasses

2 cups flour

1½ teaspoons baking soda

¼ teaspoon salt

1 teaspoon ground cinnamon

⅛ teaspoon ground cloves

½ cup water

*3 apples, peeled, halved, cored,
and cut into ⅛-inch slices*

1 cup mascarpone

½ cup heavy cream

Confectioners' sugar, for dusting

Clear Lady Apple Chips (see Appendices)

METHOD To make the cake: Cook ¼ cup of the ginger in the orange juice over low heat for 3 minutes, or until the juice is warm. Remove from the heat, cover, and steep for 30 minutes. Strain through a fine-mesh sieve and discard the ginger. Add enough milk to the orange juice to total ¾ cup of liquid, then add the brandy and vinegar. Cream the butter and ⅓ cup of the granulated sugar until light and fluffy. Add the eggs and continue beating until they are fully incorporated. Add the molasses and beat until well mixed. Sift together the flour, baking soda, salt, cinnamon, and cloves. Alternately add the dry ingredients and the orange juice mixture to the batter, mixing well after each addition. Pour the batter into a greased, floured, parchment-lined 9 by 9-inch pan and bake at 350 degrees for 25 to 30 minutes, or until a toothpick inserted in the center of the cake comes out clean. When cooled, cut the cake into 2½-inch squares and use a round cutter to cut a 1-inch hole in the center of each piece.

To make the apples and apple-ginger sauce: Cook 2 cups of the granulated sugar and the water in a medium, heavy-bottomed sauté pan over medium heat for 10 minutes, or until golden brown and caramelized. Add the apple slices and simmer gently for 3 minutes. Remove the apples, set aside, and add the remaining ¼ cup ginger to the pan. Cook for 10 minutes, or until reduced by half. Strain through a fine-mesh sieve and discard the ginger.

To make the filling: Whip the mascarpone, cream, and the remaining 2 tablespoons granulated sugar until stiff peaks form.

ASSEMBLY Lightly dust each plate with confectioners' sugar and set a piece of cake in the center. Fill the hole in the cake with the mascarpone mixture and top with some of the warmed apples. Spoon some of the mascarpone on top of the apples and stand 2 Clear Lady Apple Chips in the mascarpone. Drizzle the ginger-apple sauce around the plate.

Frozen Espresso Ice Cream Bomb with Vanilla-Rum Anglaise Emulsion

This bomb takes a little bit of work, but the results are well worth it. Fortunately, most of it can be done in advance. As if the Espresso and Bittersweet Chocolate Ice Creams were not an intense enough treat, an Espresso Praline pushes this preparation over the top. Sautéed pieces of bananas and sating Vanilla-Rum Anglaise Emulsion round out this dessert with playful elegance.

Serves 8

¼ cup milk

4 tablespoons unsalted butter

2 ounces white chocolate, chopped

¾ cup cake flour

1 teaspoon baking powder

3 eggs

5 egg yolks

¾ cup plus 1 tablespoon sugar

Espresso Ice Cream (recipe follows)

Bittersweet Chocolate Ice Cream (recipe follows)

2 bananas, scooped into Parisienne balls

White Chocolate Glaze (recipe follows)

Espresso Praline (recipe follows)

Vanilla-Rum Anglaise Emulsion (recipe follows)

Chocolate Sauce (see Appendices)

1 tablespoon unsweetened cocoa, for dusting

METHOD To make the cake: Heat the milk and 2 tablespoons of the butter until the milk starts to boil. Pour over the chocolate and set aside. Sift together the flour and baking powder and set aside. In a double boiler over barely simmering water, whisk together the eggs, egg yolks, and ¾ cup of the sugar until the mixture is doubled in volume and the whisk leaves a trail. Remove from the heat. Fold together the chocolate, egg, and flour mixtures and pour into a parchment-lined, buttered, and floured half sheet pan. Bake at 350 degrees for 13 to 15 minutes, or until the cake springs back when lightly pressed. Remove from the oven, cool, and cut into circles the size of the bomb molds.

To make the ice cream bombs: Line 8 bomb molds or small bowls (2- to 3-ounce capacity) with plastic wrap. Spread a ¾-inch layer of Espresso Ice Cream around the sides and bottom of each mold and freeze until set. Fill the center of the molds with Bittersweet Chocolate Ice Cream and freeze for at least 1 hour.

To make the bananas: Cook the remaining 2 tablespoons butter and 1 tablespoon sugar until the sugar is dissolved. Add the bananas and cook for 3 minutes, or until the bananas start to become soft. Set aside.

To glaze the bombs: Place 8 cake circles on a cooling rack over a sheet pan and top with an ice cream bomb. Pour the White Chocolate Glaze evenly over the bombs. Place the cooling rack on a second sheet pan and return the bombs to the freezer for 15 minutes to set the glaze. Scrape the glaze on the first sheet pan back into the bowl of glaze and rewarm the glaze just slightly. When the glaze on the bombs is hardened, glaze the bombs a second time and return them to the freezer until ready to serve.

ASSEMBLY Place an ice cream bomb in the center of each plate and sprinkle with the Espresso Praline. Spoon some of the Vanilla-Rum Anglaise Emulsion and Chocolate Sauce around the bomb. Arrange some of the bananas in the rings of sauce and dust with the cocoa.

Espresso Ice Cream

Yield: approximately 4 cups

3 cups heavy cream

2¼ teaspoons finely ground espresso beans

6 egg yolks

6 tablespoons sugar

METHOD Bring the cream and espresso to a boil. Remove from the heat, cover, and steep for 30 minutes. Prepare an ice water bath. Return the cream mixture to a boil. Whisk together the egg yolks and sugar. Slowly pour in some of the hot cream to temper the yolks. Pour the egg mixture into the cream and cook for 2 to 3 minutes, or until the mixture coats the back of a spoon and steam rises from the top. Strain through a fine-mesh sieve and cool over the ice water bath, stirring occasionally, until chilled. Freeze in an ice cream machine and keep frozen until ready to use.

Bittersweet Chocolate Ice Cream

Yield: approximately 3 cups

1½ cups heavy cream

½ cup milk

4 egg yolks

2 tablespoons sugar

4 ounces bittersweet chocolate, chopped

METHOD Prepare an ice water bath. Bring the cream and milk to a boil. Whisk together the egg yolks and sugar and slowly pour in some of the hot cream to temper the yolks. Pour the egg mixture into the cream and cook for 2 to 3 minutes, or until the mixture coats the back of a spoon and steam rises from the top. Pour the hot mixture

continued page 176

over the chocolate and whisk until the chocolate is completely melted. Strain through a fine-mesh sieve and cool over the ice water bath, stirring occasionally, until chilled. Freeze in an ice cream machine and keep frozen until ready to use.

White Chocolate Glaze

Yield: approximately 3 cups

1 cup heavy cream
1¹/₂ tablespoons corn syrup
24 ounces white chocolate, chopped

METHOD Bring the cream and corn syrup to a boil. Place the chocolate in a double boiler over barely simmering water. Pour the hot cream over the chocolate and stir until the chocolate is completely melted. Keep in a warm place until ready to use.

Espresso Praline

Yield: approximately ¹/₂ cup

¹/₄ cup sugar
2 tablespoons water
2 tablespoons finely ground espresso beans

METHOD Cook the sugar and water in a small sauté pan over medium-high heat for 5 minutes, or until the syrup is golden brown and caramelized. Add the espresso and pour the mixture onto a Silpat-lined or nonstick sheet pan. Let cool and finely chop.

Vanilla-Rum Anglaise Emulsion

Yield: approximately 1¹/₂ cups

1 cup heavy cream
Pulp and pod of 1 vanilla bean
2 egg yolks
2 tablespoons sugar
2 tablespoons rum

METHOD Bring the cream and vanilla pulp and pod to a boil. Cover and steep for 30 minutes. Prepare an ice water bath. Return the cream to a boil. Whisk together the egg yolks and sugar. Slowly pour in some of the hot cream to temper the yolks. Pour the egg mixture into the cream and cook for 2 to 3 minutes, or until the mixture coats the back of a spoon and steam rises from the top. Strain through a fine-mesh sieve and add the rum. Cool in the ice water bath, stirring occasionally, until chilled. Just prior to serving, mix with a handheld blender until frothy.

Whole Wheat Carrot Cake with Black Walnut Praline and Carrot Sorbet

This dessert is at once rustic and refined. It is highlighted by the moist carrot cake, which is strewn with heavenly, exotic black walnuts. This cake can be served warm or at room temperature, and it can be baked in individual servings or as a larger, family-style serving. The carrot sorbet provides a light, pure carrot flavor that delightfully reinforces the flavors in the cake. Slices of pear inside and under the cake add a complementary fruitiness. In all, this dish has a sublime earthiness, but the flavors come together for absolute refinement.

Serves 6

4 *eggs*

$^1/_4$ *cup oil*

$1^1/_4$ *cups plus 3 tablespoons sugar*

$^1/_2$ *teaspoon salt*

$^1/_2$ *cup bread flour*

$1^1/_2$ *cups whole-wheat flour*

$1^1/_2$ *tablespoons ground cinnamon*

$^3/_4$ *teaspoon baking soda*

$^1/_4$ *teaspoon baking powder*

2 *cups shredded carrots*

$^1/_2$ *cup black currants*

$^1/_2$ *cup diced fresh pineapple*

4 *large pears, peeled*

1 *large carrot*

$^2/_3$ *cup freshly squeezed orange juice*

$^1/_2$ *cup Simple Syrup (see Appendices)*

3 *tablespoons unsalted butter*

$^1/_4$ *cup freshly squeezed lemon juice*

Carrot Sorbet (recipe follows)

$^1/_2$ *cup Black Walnut Praline (see Appendices)*

METHOD To make the cake: Whip the eggs to the ribbon stage. Add the oil, $1^1/_4$ cups of the sugar, and salt and mix well. Sift together the dry ingredients, add to the batter, and mix well. Fold in the carrots, currants, and pineapple. Cut 2 of the pears in vertical $^1/_8$-inch-thick slices, avoiding the core. Cut the slices into at least twelve 2-inch circles. Fill six $2^1/_2$-inch ring molds one-quarter of the way full of batter. Top with a pear slice and fill to half full with batter. Top with another pear slice and fill the mold three-quarters of the way full of batter. Bake at 375 degrees for 20 minutes, or until the cake springs back when gently pressed in the center. Let cool and cut each cake in half vertically.

To make the candied carrots for garnish: Shred the whole carrot into $^1/_{16}$-inch julienne (a zester works well) and cook in the orange juice and Simple Syrup for 20 to 30 minutes, or until the liquid is syrupy and the carrots are candied.

To make the sautéed pear slices: Cut the remaining pears in $^1/_4$-inch wedges, removing the core. Cook the butter until brown, add the pear slices, and cook the slices on one side for 2 minutes. Add the remaining 3 tablespoons sugar and the lemon juice, turn the pears, and cook for 3 minutes, or until tender.

ASSEMBLY Place some of the sautéed pears in the center of each plate. Drizzle the juice from the pan around the plate. Arrange 2 cake halves on top of the pears and place a scoop of Carrot Sorbet in front of the cake. Sprinkle the candied carrot on the cake and around the plate. Sprinkle the Black Walnut Praline around the plate.

Carrot Sorbet

Yield: approximately 2 cups

$^1/_2$ *cup fresh carrot juice*

$^1/_2$ *cup freshly squeezed orange juice*

$^1/_4$ *cup water*

$^3/_4$ *cup chopped carrots*

$^1/_4$ *cup sugar*

2 *tablespoons corn syrup*

METHOD Combine all of the ingredients in a medium saucepan and bring to a boil. Reduce the heat to medium and simmer for 15 minutes, or until the carrots are tender. Purée the mixture for 2 minutes, or until smooth. Strain through a fine-mesh sieve and refrigerate for 1 hour. Freeze in an ice cream machine. Keep frozen until ready to use.

Espresso Pound Cake with Turkish Coffee Ice Cream and Warm Mango Compote

This simple pound cake has an exotic, sexy aroma and flavor, and although its texture is firm, it is also delicate. A pungent, heady Turkish Coffee Ice Cream adds richness and further emphasizes the cardamom flavor. The cake stands upright on the mangoes for a touch of whimsy. If the flavors in this dessert seem too much for you, try substituting vanilla ice cream for a less intense flavor.

Serves 6

1 cup unsalted butter

1½ cups sugar

4 eggs

2 cups cake flour

1 teaspoon baking powder

¼ teaspoon salt

3 tablespoons ground espresso beans

2 teaspoons pure vanilla extract

3 cardamom pods, toasted

1 ripe mango, peeled and sliced

¾ cup Simple Syrup (see Appendices)

¼ cup freshly squeezed lime juice

Turkish Coffee Ice Cream (recipe follows)

METHOD To make the pound cake: Cream the butter and sugar in a large bowl using an electric mixer fitted with the paddle attachment. Add the eggs one at a time, mixing thoroughly after each addition. Sift together the flour, baking powder, and salt, add to the batter, and mix completely. Add the coffee and vanilla extract and stir until well combined. Pour into a parchment-lined, buttered 7½ by 3½-inch loaf pan (4½- to 5-cup capacity) and bake at 350 degrees for about 1 hour, or until a wooden skewer inserted in the center comes out almost clean. (A few crumbs may still cling to the skewer.) Remove the cake from the pan and cool on a wire rack. Trim the ends from the pound cake and cut into six ¾-inch slices. Cut a 1-inch round hole in the center of each piece.

To make the mango compote: Crush the cardamom pods with a mortar and pestle. Heat the mango slices, cardamom, Simple Syrup, and lime juice until just warm.

ASSEMBLY Spoon some of the mango slices and syrup in the center of each plate. Lightly brush one side of the pound cake slices with the syrup from the mangoes. Place 2 small scoops of Turkish Coffee Ice Cream on opposite sides of the hole and press the scoops together gently to meet in the center. Place the cake upright on the mangoes and serve immediately.

Turkish Coffee Ice Cream

Yield: 1 quart

4 cardamom pods, toasted

3 cups heavy cream

2¼ teaspoons finely ground espresso beans

6 egg yolks

9 tablespoons sugar

METHOD Crush the cardamom with a mortar and pestle. Bring the cream, coffee, and cardamom to a boil. Remove from the heat, cover, and steep for 30 minutes. Prepare an ice water bath. Return the cream mixture to a boil. Whisk together the egg yolks and sugar and slowly whisk some of the hot cream into the eggs to temper the yolks. Pour the eggs back into the cream and cook over medium heat for 2 to 3 minutes, or until the mixture coats the back of a spoon and steam begins to rise from the top. Strain through a fine-mesh sieve and cool over the ice water bath, stirring occasionally, until chilled. Freeze in an ice cream machine and keep frozen until ready to use.

Chocolate

Chocolate is probably one of the most difficult dessert ingredients to pair with wine. It is usually more bitter than sweet, but with varying degrees of the richness that helps make it more wine-suitable. Older vintage ports, which have lost a lot of their tannin, are stunning wines for chocolate desserts. Vintages such as 1955, 1963, 1970, and 1985 are especially delicious right now. They are still rich and sweet, and they perfectly balance the bitterness of the chocolate. Late Bottled Vintage Ports are a great substitute for some of the vintage ports. They still have their youthful sweetness and richness, yet the cloying tannins of most vintage ports are almost nonexistent. ☙ Another wine that works well with chocolate is Banyuls, the Grenache-based Vin Doux Natural from Roussillon. Its raisiny "rancio" style is quite unique and has a rich peppery spiciness that is remarkable. From the New World vineyards of Australia and California come late harvest, fortified Zinfandels and Petite Sirahs that exhibit some of the similar characteristics as Banyuls, and are all chocolate friendly.

White Chocolate–Golden Raspberry Terrine with Oven-Dried Golden Raspberry Strips

*This is the perfect dessert for those who love white chocolate. It has a delicate richness,
as the slightly tangy golden raspberries nicely cut the creaminess of the terrine. Crispy raspberry
strips are adhered to the edges of the slices of terrine before plating for a crunchy textural effect.
The terrine can be made a day in advance and then sliced just before serving. Red raspberries
or strawberries can be used in place of the golden raspberries with fine results.*

Serves 12

2 cups heavy cream

1¹/₂ teaspoons lemon zest

8 ounces white chocolate, chopped

5 cups golden raspberries

1 egg white

¹/₂ cup plus 2 teaspoons sugar

2 cups red raspberries

¹/₄ cup water

METHOD To make the ganache: Bring the cream and lemon zest to a boil. Remove from the heat, cover, and steep for 30 minutes. Prepare an ice water bath. Return the cream mixture to a boil. Strain over the chopped chocolate, stirring occasionally, until the chocolate is melted. Cool over the ice water bath until chilled, whisking every few minutes to keep the chocolate from separating from the cream. Refrigerate overnight.

Whip the ganache until it forms stiff peaks and refrigerate until ready to use. Lightly oil the inside of a 14-inch-long, triangular terrine mold (or other 4-cup mold) and line with plastic wrap. Fold 2 cups of the golden raspberries into the cream, pour the mixture into the mold, and freeze for at least 6 hours. Cutting through the plastic wrap, slice the terrine into ¹/₂-inch slices. Remove the plastic wrap.

To make the strips: Purée 2 cups of the golden raspberries with the egg white for 2 minutes, or until smooth. Strain through a fine-mesh sieve and spread an even layer ¹/₈ inch thick onto a Silpat-lined or non-stick sheet pan. Sprinkle with 2 teaspoons of the sugar and bake at 225 degrees for 45 minutes, or until dry. Remove from the oven and, while still hot, cut ¹/₂-inch strips using a pizza cutter. Gently lift the strips from the pan and transfer to a counter or other flat surface to cool. Break the tuiles into pieces 1 inch longer than the sides of the terrine mold.

To make the sauce: Cook the red raspberries with the remaining ¹/₂ cup sugar and the water until the sugar dissolves. Purée for 2 minutes, or until smooth.

For the garnish: Slice the remaining 1 cup golden raspberries in quarters.

ASSEMBLY Place a slice of terrine in the center of each plate. Place a dried raspberry strip along each side of the terrine slices, allowing them to extend past each corner. Spoon the red raspberry sauce around the terrine and sprinkle with the golden raspberry quarters.

Individual Chocolate Charlotte with Strawberry-Ginger Sauce

*When you need that show-stopping dessert, this is it! These individual charlottes take
a little assembly time, but the result is worth it. Chocolate, ginger, strawberries, and macadamia nuts
come together for a sublime combination of flavors and textures. Raspberries or cherries
can be substituted for the strawberries for interesting flavor variations.*

Serves 4

1 1/2 cups heavy cream

6 ounces milk chocolate, chopped

*6 tablespoons Preserved Ginger, chopped,
syrup reserved (see Appendices)*

1/2 cup small-diced peeled ginger

2 cups Simple Syrup (see Appendices)

1/2 cup cornstarch

1/4 cup cocoa

1 cup bread flour

6 eggs, separated

3/4 cup plus 3 tablespoons granulated sugar

Dash of freshly squeezed lemon juice

Confectioners' sugar, for dusting

2 ounces bittersweet chocolate, tempered

*1/2 cup Macadamia Nut Praline, chopped
(see Appendices)*

Strawberry-Ginger Sauce (recipe follows)

Chocolate-Ginger Sauce (recipe follows)

METHOD To make the mousse: Bring the cream to a boil, pour over the milk chocolate, and stir until the chocolate is completely melted. Refrigerate overnight.

Whip the mousse until it forms stiff peaks, fold in 3 tablespoons of the Preserved Ginger syrup and the chopped Preserved Ginger. Spoon the mixture into 4 lightly oiled 2 1/2-inch-diameter by 1 1/2-inch-high ring molds and refrigerate until ready to use.

To make the diced ginger: Blanch the ginger in boiling water and drain. Repeat the process 3 times. Place the blanched ginger in a small pan with the Simple Syrup and simmer for 45 minutes.

To make the ladyfingers: Sift together the cornstarch, cocoa, and flour. Whip the egg yolks with 5 tablespoons of the granulated sugar until light and creamy. Whip the egg whites, 5 tablespoons of the granulated sugar, and a drop of the lemon juice until foamy and tripled in volume. Gradually add the remaining 5 tablespoons granulated sugar and whip until stiff peaks form. Fold the egg yolk mixture into the egg whites, and then fold in the dry ingredients. Spoon into a pastry bag and pipe into 1/4 by 2-inch strips on a parchment-lined sheet pan. Bake at 425 degrees for 4 to 5 minutes, or until set. Remove from the oven and let cool. Dust with confectioners' sugar.

To make the chocolate bands: Cut eight 1/2 by 12-inch strips of parchment. Wrap a parchment strip around one of the cakes and cut it to 1 inch longer than the circumference of the cake. Cut 2 strips for each cake. Place the parchment strips on the back of a sheet pan and use an offset spatula to spread the tempered bittersweet chocolate. Place in a cool location for the chocolate to set. When the chocolate begins to set, wrap a strip around the ladyfingers, pinching the ends together tightly where they meet. Do not let the ends overlap. Repeat this process with all of the strips and refrigerate the cakes to harden the chocolate. Remove the cakes from the refrigerator and carefully peel the parchment away from the chocolate. (There will be one extra for each cake, in case the chocolate cracks.)

ASSEMBLY Heat a knife in hot water and run the knife around the inside edge of the mold to loosen the mousse. Remove the mold. Place the ladyfingers vertically around the mousse, slightly overlapping each one. Place a chocolate band around the ladyfingers. Sprinkle some of the Macadamia Nut Praline on top of each cake and place a ladyfinger wrapped-mousse in the center of each plate. Spoon the Strawberry-Ginger Sauce and warm Chocolate-Ginger Sauce around the cake and sprinkle the Preserved Ginger over the sauce.

Strawberry-Ginger Sauce

Yield: 1/2 cup

1/4 cup freshly squeezed lemon juice
5 strawberries, halved
*2 tablespoons chopped Preserved Ginger,
with syrup (see Appendices)*

METHOD Purée all of the ingredients for 2 minutes, or until smooth, and strain through a fine-mesh sieve.

Chocolate-Ginger Sauce

Yield: approximately 1/2 cup

1/2 cup heavy cream
1 tablespoon chopped fresh ginger
2 ounces bittersweet chocolate, chopped

METHOD Bring the cream and ginger to a boil. Remove from the heat, cover, and let steep for 30 minutes. Return to a boil. Place the chocolate in a small saucepan. Strain the ginger-cream mixture over the chocolate and stir continuously until the chocolate is completely melted. If the sauce is too thick, thin with a little hot water. Serve warm.

Of course one can "go too far" and except in directions in which we
can go too far there is no interest in going at all; and only those who will risk
going too far can possibly find out just how far one can go.

— T. S. Elliot

German Chocolate Cake Terrine with Coconut Sauce and Toasted Coconut

This terrine is an interpretation of a classic. It is festive and gives people the sense that something special was done for them. As a child, one of my favorite desserts was German chocolate cake; some things never change. The chocolate and the buttery coconut combine for true bliss. The creamy coconut sauce provides an ethereal richness. More sinful still would be to add coconut ice cream.

Serves 8

3 tablespoons unsweetened cocoa

2 tablespoons flour

⅛ teaspoon salt

6 eggs, separated

2 cups sugar

1½ teaspoons pure vanilla extract

3½ cups heavy cream

3 cups toasted coconut

⅓ cup freshly squeezed orange juice

¼ cup corn syrup

7 ounces bittersweet chocolate, melted

1 tablespoon unsalted butter, melted and cooled

1 cup half-and-half

1 tablespoon orange zest

1 egg yolk

METHOD To make the cake: Sift together the cocoa, flour, and salt. Whip the 6 egg yolks until light in color. Add ¾ cup of the sugar 1 tablespoon at a time, mixing well between additions. Add the vanilla extract and mix well. Add the dry ingredients and mix just until combined.

Whip the egg whites to stiff peaks. Stir one-quarter of the whites into the batter to loosen the mixture. Fold the remaining egg whites into the batter in three separate additions to avoid breaking down the egg whites. Pour the batter into a parchment-lined, buttered half sheet pan and bake at 350 degrees for 20 minutes, or until the cake springs back when lightly pressed and starts to pull away from the sides of the pan. Remove from the oven, let cool, and invert onto a board. Remove the parchment.

To make the filling: Cook 3 cups of the cream, ¾ cup of the toasted coconut, the orange juice, ¾ cup of the sugar, and the corn syrup over medium-low heat for 30 to 40 minutes, or until reduced to about 1½ cups. Prepare an ice water bath. Strain the cream mixture through a fine-mesh sieve and chill over the ice water bath, stirring occasionally. Fold in 1¼ cups of the coconut.

To make the ganache: Whisk together the melted chocolate, melted butter, and the remaining ½ cup of cream.

To assemble the cake: Line a 2¼-inch-wide by 1½-inch-high by 8-inch-long terrine mold with plastic wrap. Trim the sides from the cake and cut the cake into 7 strips the same width and length as the mold. Place a layer of cake in the mold and evenly spread about 3 tablespoons of the coconut filling on the cake. Continue layering, ending with the seventh cake strip. Wrap the terrine tightly with the plastic wrap. Place the cake in the freezer for 1 hour, or until very firm.

Remove the cake from the mold and cut the terrine into four 2-inch-thick pieces. Set the pieces on their side so the layers are vertical. Cut each piece diagonally to form 2 triangles. Stand the triangles on end with the layers running vertically and line them up with the cake sides close together. Use the remaining coconut filling to adhere each of the 4 triangles together. Brush off any stray crumbs and place the cakes on a cooling rack over a sheet pan. Spoon the ganache over the angled sides of the cakes (the ganache that runs off the cakes can be taken off the sheet pan and reused). Refrigerate the cakes to harden the ganache. Reglaze with the remaining ganache if there are any uncovered spots. Trim off any glaze that may have run onto the front or back of the cakes. Cut each cake into two 1-inch-thick slices across the center.

To make the coconut sauce: Bring the half-and-half, ¾ cup of the coconut, and the orange zest to a boil. Whisk together the remaining egg yolk and ½ cup sugar and slowly pour in some of the hot cream to temper the egg. Pour the egg mixture into the cream and continue cooking for 2 to 3 minutes, or until the mixture coats the back of a spoon and steam rises from the top. Strain through a fine-mesh sieve.

ASSEMBLY Place a slice of cake in the center of each plate. Drizzle the coconut sauce around the plate and sprinkle the remaining ¼ cup coconut around the plates.

Chocolate Devil's Food Cake with a Candied Carrot Lattice and Cardamom Ice Cream

This Chocolate Devil's Food Cake gets its interesting flavor and texture from the carrot purée in the batter. The sweet, earthy flavor of the carrot highlights the musty, sensual flavor of the chocolate and helps makes the cake especially moist. The ice cream adds a glorious richness, and the flavor of cardamom is exciting and exotic. The crispy carrot lattice is playful and provides a textural contrast to the smooth ice cream and melt-away cake. Try substituting beets for the carrots for an interesting variation.

Serves 6

1/3 cup canola oil

Pulp and pod of 1 vanilla bean

1 1/4 cups sugar

1 egg

1/2 cup cooked carrot purée

1/2 cup plus 1 tablespoon flour

1/2 teaspoon baking soda

Pinch of salt

1/3 cup unsweetened cocoa

2 ounces bittersweet chocolate, melted

1/4 cup crème fraîche

1/3 cup water

12 baby carrots, peeled and cooked

Candied Carrot Lattices (recipe follows)

Cardamom Ice Cream (recipe follows)

METHOD To make the cake: Cook the oil and vanilla pulp and pod over medium heat for 8 minutes, remove from the heat, and let cool. Remove and discard the vanilla bean and pour the oil into a mixing bowl. Add 1/2 cup of the sugar. Using an electric mixer fitted with the paddle attachment, beat the oil and sugar for 5 minutes. Add the egg and carrot purée and mix until thoroughly combined. Sift together the flour, baking soda, salt, and cocoa and blend into the sugar mixture. Add the chocolate and crème fraîche and mix well. Place 6 buttered 2 1/2-inch-diameter by 1 1/2-inch-high ring molds on a sheet pan and fill halfway with the batter. Bake at 350 degrees for 20 to 25 minutes, or until a toothpick inserted in the center comes out clean. Let cool on the pan and then remove the ring molds.

To caramelize the carrots: Cook the remaining 3/4 cup sugar and the water over medium-high heat for 10 minutes, or until the sugar is golden brown and caramelized. Add the carrots, stir until they are thoroughly coated, and remove from the heat.

ASSEMBLY Place one of the cakes in the center of each plate. Spoon 2 baby carrots onto each plate and drizzle the caramel from cooking the carrots around the plate. Lean a Candied Carrot Lattice on the side of each cake and top with a quenelle of Cardamom Ice Cream.

Candied Carrot Lattices

Yield: approximately 6 lattices

3 large carrots, peeled

2 cups water

3/4 cup sugar

METHOD Using a vegetable peeler, peel the carrots into strips the length of the carrot. Bring the water and sugar to a boil, add the carrot strips, and simmer over medium heat for 25 minutes. Carefully remove the strips and weave them into 6 individual lattices on a Silpat-lined or nonstick sheet pan. Bake at 225 degrees for 1 1/2 to 2 hours, or until the carrots are crisp. Remove the lattices to a counter or another flat surface to cool.

Cardamom Ice Cream

Yield: approximately 3 cups

10 cardamom pods

2 cups heavy cream

1 1/2 tablespoons orange zest

4 egg yolks

1/4 cup sugar

METHOD Toast the cardamom pods in the oven at 350 degrees for 10 minutes. Let cool and then grind the pods in a spice mill. Bring the cream, cardamom, and orange zest to a boil. Remove from the heat, cover, and steep for 30 minutes. Prepare an ice water bath. Return the cream mixture to a boil. Whisk together the egg yolks and sugar and slowly pour in some of the hot cream to temper the eggs. Pour the egg mixture into the cream and cook for 2 to 3 minutes, or until the mixture coats the back of a spoon and steam rises from the top. Strain through a fine-mesh sieve and place over the ice water bath, stirring occasionally, until chilled. Freeze in an ice cream machine and keep frozen until ready to use.

Chocolate Brioche–English Toffee Bread Pudding

~~~~~~

This dessert is for the hard-core chocolate lover. The dense, moist bread pudding literally makes your head buzz when you take a bite. The English toffee adds a great textural note and a sensual, enriching caramel flavor. The glazed bananas add more fabulous flavor and a little crunchiness. The preparation can be done in advance and the dessert can be reheated just before serving, or it can be served at room temperature.

Serves 12

3 cups plus 1 tablespoon heavy cream

3 eggs

3 egg yolks

1/2 cup plus 2 tablespoons sugar

9 ounces bittersweet chocolate, chopped

Chocolate Brioche (recipe follows)

English Toffee (recipe follows)

2 tablespoons unsalted butter

2 large bananas, peeled and sliced 1/4 inch thick

1/2 cup milk

METHOD To make the pudding: Bring 3 cups of the cream to a boil. Whisk together the eggs, egg yolks, and 1/2 cup of the sugar. Slowly pour in some of the hot cream to temper the eggs. Pour the egg mixture into the cream and cook for 2 to 3 minutes, or until the sugar is dissolved. Pour the cream mixture over 3 ounces of the chocolate and whisk until the chocolate is completely melted. Place the Chocolate Brioche pieces in a large bowl and pour in the cream mixture. Allow the brioche to soak, turning occasionally, until all of the liquid is absorbed. Fold in the remaining 6 ounces of chocolate and 1 cup of the English Toffee. Spoon the mixture into a buttered 9 by 9-inch pan and bake at 350 degrees for 45 minutes, or until a knife inserted in the center comes out clean. Let cool for 10 minutes and cut into 2 by 3-inch pieces.

To prepare the bananas: Brown the butter in a sauté pan over medium-high heat. Toss the bananas in the remaining 2 tablespoons of sugar and cook for 2 to 3 minutes, or until they are slightly brown. Remove the bananas from the pan, turn off the heat, and pour in the remaining 1 tablespoon cream to deglaze the pan, scraping and incorporating any banana sticking to the bottom of the pan. Stir in the milk. Strain through a fine-mesh sieve and blend with a handheld blender until frothy.

ASSEMBLY Spoon some of the sautéed bananas in the center of each plate and top with a piece of bread pudding. Spoon the banana emulsion around the plate and sprinkle with the remaining pieces of English Toffee.

Chocolate Brioche

Yield: one 9 by 4-inch loaf

1 1/2 teaspoons active dry yeast

2 tablespoons warm water

2 tablespoons sugar

3 eggs

1 1/2 teaspoons salt

2 cups flour

1/4 cup unsweetened cocoa

1 cup unsalted butter, softened

METHOD Combine the yeast, water, and 1 tablespoon of the sugar and let stand for 3 minutes. Whisk together the eggs, the remaining 1 tablespoon sugar, and the salt. Add the yeast mixture and stir in the flour and cocoa. Add the butter and mix until the dough comes away from the sides of the bowl. Form into a log and place in a buttered and floured 9 by 4-inch loaf pan. Cover and let rise for 1 to 2 hours, or until almost doubled in size. Bake at 375 degrees for 35 to 45 minutes, or until golden brown. Remove the brioche from the pan and cool on a wire rack. Cut into small dice.

English Toffee

Yield: approximately 2 cups

3/4 cup sugar

6 tablespoons heavy cream

6 tablespoons unsalted butter, cubed

4 ounces bittersweet chocolate, chopped

METHOD Place the sugar and cream in a heavy saucepan over medium heat. Add the butter and bring to a boil. Allow the mixture to cook and bubble, swirling the pan as necessary, until it is a dark caramel color throughout (do not stir). Remove the pan from the heat and allow the mixture to cool and thicken slightly. Pour the mixture onto the back of a nonstick sheet pan or a lightly oiled cutting board and use a spatula to push it into a rectangular shape. When it is firm enough to cut, slice the toffee into 1/2-inch strips using a pizza cutter or a sharp knife.

Melt 3 ounces of the chocolate in a double boiler over barely simmering water until almost melted. Remove from the heat, add the remaining 1 ounce chocolate, and stir continuously until the chocolate has cooled to body temperature. Pour the chocolate over the toffee and separate the strips slightly. Let cool at room temperature for 15 minutes, or until the chocolate hardens. Cut the toffee strips into 1/4-inch-wide pieces.

Chocolate–Bing Cherry Cake with Bing Cherry Sauce

Of all the fruits that can be successfully paired with chocolate, cherries may be the best match. Their sweet flavor melds perfectly into the pungent, heady flavor of the chocolate. Cherries also have just enough acid to barely cut the fat of the chocolate. Here, the dried, chewy, slightly tart cherries are incorporated into the body of the cake, while the plump, sweet, ganache-filled poached Bing cherries are served under it, or to the side. This cake can be made in advance and served either hot or cold. Bing cherry or chocolate ice cream could be served on the side for the ultimate indulgence.

Serves 12

3 eggs

1 cup buttermilk

1 cup sour cream

1 1/4 cups sugar

1/2 cup plus 2 tablespoons unsweetened cocoa

1 cup all-purpose flour

1 cup cake flour

1 teaspoon baking soda

1 teaspoon baking powder

3/4 cup unsalted butter, melted

1/2 cup dried cherries

1 cup Sauternes

1/2 cup water

1/4 cup freshly squeezed lemon juice

2 cinnamon sticks

3 star anise

48 Bing cherries, pitted

Chocolate–Earl Grey Tea Ganache (recipe follows)

White Chocolate Sauce (recipe follows)

Cherry Tuiles (recipe follows)

METHOD To make the cake: Beat the eggs until they are tripled in volume. Add the buttermilk and sour cream and mix well. Sift together the sugar, cocoa, flours, baking soda, and baking powder, add to the batter, and mix well. Stir in the melted butter and fold in the dried cherries. Pour the batter into a buttered, floured, parchment-lined 9 by 13-inch pan. Bake in a water bath at 350 degrees for 25 to 35 minutes, or until the cake springs back when lightly pressed in the center. Cool slightly, invert onto a sheet pan, and invert again onto a cutting board. Let cool and cut into triangles.

To make the Bing cherry sauce: Bring the Sauternes, water, lemon juice, cinnamon, and star anise to a boil over medium heat. Add the whole cherries and return the mixture to a boil. Remove the cherries from the liquid and set aside. Return the pan to medium heat and continue cooking for 15 minutes, or until the liquid is reduced to about 2/3 cup. Add 12 cherries to the liquid, purée for 1 minute, and strain through a fine-mesh sieve.

To prepare the cherries: Fill the remaining 36 cherries with the Chocolate–Earl Grey Tea Ganache.

ASSEMBLY Spoon a ring of White Chocolate Sauce around the plate. Spoon the Bing cherry sauce in the center of the chocolate sauce ring and place 3 filled cherries in the center of the sauce. Top with a Cherry Tuile. Place a cake triangle on each tuile.

Chocolate–Earl Grey Tea Ganache

Yield: approximately 1 cup

1/2 cup heavy cream

1 tablespoon Earl Grey tea

7 ounces bittersweet chocolate, chopped

1 tablespoon unsalted butter

METHOD Bring the cream and tea to a boil. Remove from the heat, cover, and steep for 30 minutes. Return to a boil and then strain the liquid over the chocolate and butter. Whisk until smooth and refrigerate until stiff enough to pipe into the cherries.

White Chocolate Sauce

Yield: approximately 1/3 cup

3 ounces white chocolate, melted

1 to 2 tablespoons water

METHOD Whisk together the chocolate and enough water to create a sauce consistency. Keep in a warm location until ready to use.

Cherry Tuiles

Yield: 1 cup batter

1 cup pitted Bing cherries

1/4 cup water

1 egg white

METHOD Cook the cherries in the water for 5 minutes and let cool. Purée the mixture for 1 minute, add the egg white, and purée for 2 more minutes. Spoon 1 to 1 1/2 teaspoons of the batter onto a Silpat-lined or nonstick sheet pan and spread into a 3-inch circle. Repeat to form at least 12 tuiles (make extra to allow for breakage). Bake at 225 degrees for 40 minutes, or until the tuiles are dry enough to remove from the pan. Carefully lift the tuiles using a small offset spatula and place on a countertop or other flat surface to cool.

Crepe "Banana Split"

Although this does not exactly resemble the classic banana split, its origins are there.
The chewiness of the crepes gives this preparation a delightful new twist. Chocolate, mint, and
vanilla ice creams are contained within their respectively flavored crepes and then are
placed on top of glazed bananas, pineapples, and cherries. Bittersweet chocolate and
pineapple-caramel sauces are drizzled around the crepes and topped with chopped peanuts.
It takes some work to prepare all of this, but sometimes it's fun to go the extra mile.

Serves 6

Vanilla Ice Cream (recipe follows)

Mint Ice Cream (recipe follows)

Milk Chocolate Ice Cream (see Appendices)

1/2 cup dried sour cherries, chopped

1/4 cup freshly squeezed orange juice

1 cup granulated sugar

1/4 cup water

*18 thin slices fresh pineapple,
cut in half circles*

2 bananas, peeled

1/2 cup heavy cream

1 tablespoon confectioners' sugar

Basic Crepes (recipe follows)

*1/2 cup packed fresh mint leaves, blanched
and shocked*

1 tablespoon unsweetened cocoa, sifted

Pulp and pod of 1 vanilla bean

3 vanilla beans, cut into 18 very thin strips

Chocolate Sauce (see Appendices)

6 tablespoons chopped peanuts

METHOD To prepare the ice creams: Put 6 small scoops of each of the 3 ice creams on a pan and place in the coldest part of the freezer.

To prepare the cherries: Cook the cherries and orange juice until simmering. Remove from the heat and let cool in the pan.

To prepare the pineapple: Combine 3/4 cup of the granulated sugar with the water in a medium sauté pan and cook over medium-high heat for 10 minutes, or until the sugar is golden brown and caramelized. Add the pineapple slices, stir until coated, and set aside in the syrup until ready to use.

To prepare the bananas: Cut the bananas into 1/4-inch-thick slices, place on a sheet

pan, and sprinkle with the remaining 1/4 cup granulated sugar. Caramelize the sugar until golden brown using a blowtorch.

To make the whipped cream: Whip the cream with the confectioners' sugar until it forms stiff peaks. Refrigerate until needed.

To make the crepes: Divide the Basic Crepes recipe into 3 portions. Add the mint leaves to one portion and purée for 1 minute. Add the cocoa to another portion and whisk until completely incorporated. Add the vanilla pulp to the remaining portion and whisk until completely combined.

Heat a 5-inch nonstick sauté pan or crepe pan and lightly coat with oil. Pour 2 table-spoons of batter into the pan, swirling it to evenly spread the batter. Cook for 1 minute, flip over, cook for 30 seconds, and remove from the pan. Repeat this process until there are at least 6 of each type of crepe. Stack the crepes separately by types.

ASSEMBLY Place a small scoop of Vanilla Ice cream in the center of each vanilla crepe and tie with a strip of the vanilla

bean. Place a small scoop of Mint Ice Cream in the center of each mint crepe and a small scoop of Chocolate Ice Cream in the center of each chocolate crepe. Tie each crepe with a strip of the vanilla bean.

Place some of the caramelized bananas in the center of each plate. Spoon some of the cherries on one side of the bananas and 3 slices of pineapple on the other side. Place the stuffed Vanilla Crepe on top of the pineapple, the Mint Crepe on top of the bananas, and the Chocolate Crepe on top of the cherries. Drizzle the Chocolate Sauce and caramel from cooking the pineapple around the plate. Sprinkle the sauces with the peanuts and place a spoonful of whipped cream next to the pineapple.

Vanilla Ice Cream

Yield: approximately 3 cups

2 cups heavy cream
Pulp and pod of 1 vanilla bean
4 egg yolks
6 tablespoons sugar

METHOD Prepare an ice water bath. Bring the cream and vanilla pulp and pod to a boil. Whisk together the egg yolks and sugar and slowly pour in some of the cream to temper the eggs. Pour the egg mixture into the cream and cook for 2 to 3 minutes, or until the mixture coats the back of a spoon and steam rises from the top. Strain through a fine-mesh sieve and cool in the ice water bath, stirring occasionally, until chilled. Freeze in an ice cream machine and keep frozen until ready to use.

Mint Ice Cream

Yield: approximately 3 cups

2 cups heavy cream
1 cup packed fresh mint, blanched, shocked, squeezed dry, and chopped
4 egg yolks
6 tablespoons sugar
1/2 cup packed fresh spinach, blanched, shocked, squeezed dry, and chopped

METHOD Prepare an ice water bath. Bring the cream and mint to a boil. Whisk together the egg yolks and sugar and slowly

pour in some of the cream to temper the eggs. Pour the egg mixture into the cream and cook for 2 to 3 minutes, or until the mixture coats the back of a spoon and steam rises from the top. Pour the mixture into a blender, add the spinach, and purée for 2 minutes, or until smooth. Strain through a fine-mesh sieve and cool in the ice water bath, stirring occasionally, until chilled. Freeze in an ice cream machine and keep frozen until ready to use.

Basic Crepes

Yield: about 24 crepes

1 1/4 cups flour
3 tablespoons sugar
Pinch of salt
4 eggs
2 egg yolks
6 tablespoons unsalted butter, melted
2 cups milk, warm

METHOD Purée all of the ingredients for 2 minutes and strain through a fine-mesh sieve.

Chocolate Tortellini with White Bean Ice Cream and Blood Orange–Caramel Sauce

Chocolate and white beans may seem an odd combination, but the mildness of the beans contrasts with and elevates the pungent ganache-filled chocolate tortellini. The puréed beans in the ice cream base lend a special satiny quality to the finished dessert, which is even further highlighted by the satisfying chewiness of the pasta. The sweet-tart caramel sauce provides a remarkable balance to both the chocolate and the white bean flavors, and the tiny leaves of mint offer a whimsical cleansing note.

Serves 8

3 tablespoons heavy cream
1 tablespoon orange zest
3 ounces bittersweet chocolate, chopped
3 tablespoons unsalted butter
1 tablespoon cocoa
1 tablespoon hot water
1 tablespoon melted bittersweet chocolate
1 egg, at room temperature
3/4 cup semolina flour
1/4 cup plus 2 tablespoons sugar
1 egg, beaten
4 blood oranges
1/4 cup water
1 cup freshly squeezed blood orange juice
White Bean Ice Cream (recipe follows)
1 1/2 tablespoons tiny mint leaves
Mint Syrup (see Appendices)

METHOD To make the ganache: Stir the cream, orange zest, chopped chocolate, and butter in a double boiler over barely simmering water until melted. Strain through a fine-mesh sieve and refrigerate for 2 hours, or until firm.

To make the pasta: Combine the cocoa and hot water and stir to make a paste. Place the cocoa mixture, the melted chocolate, egg, semolina flour, and the 2 tablespoons sugar in an electric mixer fitted with a dough hook and blend for 5 minutes, or until the ingredients are combined. Remove the dough from the mixer and knead by hand until smooth, adding a little flour if the dough is too sticky. Cover the dough with plastic wrap and refrigerate for 1 hour. Roll the dough out to a 1/16-inch-thick piece and cut into twenty-four 2 1/2-inch squares.

To make the tortellini: Place about 1 teaspoon of the ganache in the center of each square. Brush 2 of the edges with the egg, fold over the square to form a triangle, and pinch the edges to seal. Pull the 2 points on the long side together and pinch firmly to form the tortellini. Drop the tortellini into simmering water for 3 minutes, or until they float. Drain and set aside.

To make the sauce: Cut the tops and bottoms off the blood oranges. Using a sharp knife, cut the peels off the oranges, removing all of the white pith. Cut the oranges on both sides of each membrane and remove the orange segments. Cook the remaining 1/4 cup sugar and the 1/4 cup water in a small, heavy-bottomed sauté pan over medium heat for 5 minutes, or until golden brown and caramelized. Add the orange juice and cook for 2 to 3 minutes, or until the mixture is smooth and slightly reduced. Remove the pan from the heat. Add the orange segments, cook for 30 seconds, and remove to a bowl.

ASSEMBLY Arrange the orange segments in the center of each plate and drizzle with the orange sauce. Top with a quenelle of White Bean Ice Cream. Place 3 tortellini around the ice cream and sprinkle the mint leaves around the plate. Drizzle the Mint Syrup around the tortellini.

White Bean Ice Cream

Yield: approximately 3 cups

1/2 cup heavy cream
1 cup milk
4 egg yolks
1/4 cup sugar
1/2 cup cooked white beans
1/2 cup freshly squeezed orange juice
1/4 cup Simple Syrup (see Appendices)

METHOD Prepare an ice water bath. Bring the cream and milk to a boil. Whisk together the egg yolks and sugar and slowly pour in some of the hot cream to temper the eggs. Pour the eggs into the cream and cook over low heat for 2 to 3 minutes, or until the mixture coats the back of a spoon and steam rises from the top. Blend the beans, orange juice, and syrup, then add the cream mixture and purée until combined. Strain through a fine-mesh sieve, chill over the ice water bath, and freeze in an ice cream machine. Keep frozen until ready to use.

Nothing more excellent or valuable than wine has ever been granted by the gods to man. – SOCRATES

Château d'Yquem

Château d'Yquem is one of the most, if not *the* most sought-after wine in the world. Some say this decadent wine is made by the divine intervention over man and nature. Its ethereal bouquet of honeysuckle, pears, peaches, and delicate spice make this wine a wonderful dessert all on its own. Elements such as figs, nuts, stone fruits, and blue cheese have classically been served with Yquem, and only the desserts that retain these intrinsic characteristics, which accentuate the wine's flavors, are worthy of its glory. The recipes in this chapter have incorporated these elements, bringing together the vibrant flavors of nature in the food and the wine. Like all wines, Château d'Yquem varies from vintage to vintage and different vintages may be used for different styles of dessert. Younger vintages of Yquem are phenomenal with especially rich custards and sabayons, whereas the older vintages, which have shed some of their sweetness, have stronger nut and dried-fruit flavors that are a great match for elegant fruit and nut tarts.

Three-Point Peach Tart with Peach Compote and Preserved Ginger

This tart may appear somewhat rustic, but it is actually a very elegant dessert.
The Cream Cheese Dough melts in your mouth almost like puff pastry, yet it maintains
a nice crispiness. The entire concoction is enhanced by the addition of the ginger and sage.
This tart is fairly versatile: it not only works well with a variety of fruits—plums, figs,
apples, pears, or strawberries—but it can be served hot out of the oven or at room temperature.
When served warm, the peaches explode like molten jam. A scoop of ice cream
can be added to provide additional richness.

Serves 6

Cream Cheese Dough (see Appendices)

4 white peaches

3 tablespoons granulated sugar

⅛ teaspoon ground cinnamon

¼ cup crème fraîche

1 egg, beaten

Confectioners' sugar, for dusting

¼ cup Simple Syrup (see Appendices)

¼ cup freshly squeezed lemon juice

*2 tablespoons Preserved Ginger
(see Appendices)*

2 tablespoons tiny fresh sage leaves

METHOD To make the tart shells: Roll out the Cream Cheese Dough to ⅛ inch thick and cut into six 5-inch circles. Refrigerate on a parchment-lined sheet pan for 15 minutes.

To make the filling: Peel and dice 2 of the peaches and toss together with 2 tablespoons of the granulated sugar, the cinnamon, and crème fraîche.

To assemble the tarts: Brush the dough lightly with the beaten egg and spoon a generous tablespoon of the filling in the center of each circle. Lift up the edges of the tart and pinch 3 points of the tart about halfway to the filling to form the sides of the crust. Refrigerate for 30 minutes. Brush the edges of the crust with the egg and sprinkle lightly with the remaining 1 tablespoon granulated sugar. Pinch the dough again to make sure it is tightly sealed and freeze for 10 minutes. Remove the tarts from the freezer and immediately bake at 350 degrees for 20 to 25 minutes, or until golden brown. Let cool slightly and dust with confectioners' sugar.

To make the compote: Dice the remaining 2 peaches with the skin on, toss with the Simple Syrup and lemon juice, and warm slightly.

ASSEMBLY Spoon some of the diced peaches and juice around the plate. Place a tart in the center of each plate and sprinkle with the Preserved Ginger and sage leaves.

Whole Nectarine Confit with Château d'Yquem Granité

This dessert is a refreshing explosion of sweet fruit and icy Sauternes. The nectarine is poached until it just softens and then is filled with an easy-to-make, very satisfying Château d'Yquem Granité. This preparation is quite light, so it works perfectly as a prelude to another dessert or as a splendid ending to a light summer luncheon. Best of all, the entire preparation can be done well in advance—you merely scoop the granité into the fruit when you are ready to serve. For a twist that provides a divine headiness, try crumbling a little Stilton around the plate.

Serves 6

10 ripe nectarines

2 cups water

½ cup freshly squeezed lemon juice

1 cup sugar

Château d'Yquem Granité (recipe follows)

1 tablespoon tiny marigold petals

METHOD To make the nectarines: Peel and chop 4 of the nectarines and purée them with the water and lemon juice for 2 minutes, or until smooth. Add the sugar and pour into a saucepan. Cut the stem end from the remaining nectarines. Using a paring knife, cut around the pits. Trim a slice from the bottom of the nectarines and use the knife to loosen the pit. Push out the pit and trim the inside of the nectarine to form a generous cavity for the granité. Place the nectarines in the pot, adding additional water if they are not completely covered. Bring to a simmer and cook until the nectarines are fork-tender. (The time will vary depending on the ripeness of the nectarines.) Peel the nectarines. Reserve 1 cup of the cooking liquid for the granité and ½ cup for a sauce.

ASSEMBLY Place a whole nectarine in the center of each plate. Fill the center of each nectarine with the Château d'Yquem Granité, piling it up over the top of the fruit. Spoon some of the reserved sauce down the sides of the nectarine and onto the plate. Sprinkle the marigold leaves on the granité and around the plate.

Château d'Yquem Granité

Yield: 3 cups

1 cup Château d'Yquem

1 cup reserved cooking liquid from the nectarines

METHOD Combine all of the ingredients in a shallow pan and place in the freezer. Scrape the mixture with a spoon every 15 to 20 minutes for 2 hours, or until frozen, to form the granité.

Roasted Apricot French Toast with Sabayon and Apricot—Château d'Yquem Sauce

*Apricots are one of the best partners for Sauternes. Their profound sweet-tart flavor provides
an extraordinary foil to the sweet, unctuous wine. In this case, slightly cooked pieces
of the fruit are placed on a slice of browned, buttery brioche. An ethereal Château d'Yquem Sabayon
is spooned on and then glazed over lightly. The resulting texture and flavor combinations
will make you want to be alone with only the dessert and a glass of Château d'Yquem:
conversation or other distractions will be superfluous.*

Serves 6

Brioche Dough (see Appendices)

6 apricots

¼ cup firmly packed brown sugar

1 egg

1 cup heavy cream

⅛ teaspoon ground cinnamon

⅛ teaspoon ground nutmeg

Pulp of 1 vanilla bean

¼ cup sugar

Sabayon (recipe follows)

*Apricot—Château d'Yquem Sauce
(recipe follows)*

METHOD To make the brioche: Place the dough in a parchment-lined, buttered 7½ by 3½-inch loaf pan. Cover with plastic wrap and let rise in a warm place for 1 hour, or until doubled in size. Bake at 375 degrees for 35 to 40 minutes, or until golden brown. Remove from the pan, cool on a wire rack, and cut into six ¾-inch-thick slices. Trim the crust from the slices.

To prepare the apricots: Cut the apricots in ¼-inch wedges and toss with the brown sugar. Place on a sheet pan and bake at 325 degrees for 15 minutes, or until slightly tender. Keep warm.

To make the French toast: Whisk together the egg, cream, cinnamon, nutmeg, vanilla pulp, and sugar. Dip the brioche slices in the cream mixture. Sauté the brioche in a lightly oiled pan over medium heat for 2 minutes on each side, or until light golden brown.

ASSEMBLY Place a piece of brioche French toast in the center of each plate. Arrange the apricot wedges on the brioche and spoon 2 tablespoons of the Sabayon on top. Heat the Sabayon with a blowtorch for 10 seconds, or until browned. Drizzle some of the Apricot—Château d'Yquem Sauce around the plate.

Sabayon

Yield: ½ cup

8 egg yolks

¼ cup Simple Syrup (see Appendices)

METHOD Combine the egg yolks and Simple Syrup in a double boiler over barely simmering water. Whisk continuously for 15 minutes, or until it reaches the ribbon stage.

Apricot—Château d'Yquem Sauce

Yield: approximately 1 cup

3 apricots, pitted and chopped

⅓ cup freshly squeezed orange juice

¼ cup Simple Syrup (see Appendices)

⅓ cup Château d'Yquem

METHOD Cook the apricots in the orange juice and Simple Syrup until the apricots are tender. Pour into a blender and pulse just to combine, creating a slightly chunky texture. Stir in the Château d'Yquem and warm before serving.

You must push yourself beyond your limits at all times. – CARLOS CASTANEDA

Peach-Polenta Upside-Down Cake
with Almond Sherbet

~~~~~~

The slight graininess of the polenta in this cake gives a wonderful rustic feeling to the preparation,
and the caramelization that develops on the peach and around the top of the cake heightens that effect.
The Almond Sherbet is light but bursting with flavor, and a few pieces of candied almond
add just the right amount of crunchy texture. This cake is at its best right out of the oven;
however, it can be made several hours ahead and reheated just before serving with fine results.

Serves 12

¾ cup unsalted butter

2 cups plus 3 tablespoons sugar

3 eggs

6 egg yolks

¾ cup plus 1 tablespoon flour

½ cup plus 2 tablespoons cornmeal

¾ teaspoon baking powder

½ teaspoon salt

¾ cup water

8 small Indian red peaches

½ cup freshly squeezed lemon juice

1 cup heavy cream

¼ cup almonds, toasted

Almond Sherbet (recipe follows)

Candied Almonds (recipe follows)

METHOD To make the cake: Cream the butter and 1 cup of the sugar. Add the eggs and egg yolks one at a time, mixing thoroughly after each addition. Combine the dry ingredients in a separate bowl and add to the batter, mixing completely.

Cook ¾ cup of the sugar and ¼ cup of the water in a small, heavy-bottomed sauté pan over medium heat for 10 minutes, or until golden brown and caramelized. Wrap the bottoms of twelve 2½-inch-diameter by 1½-inch-high ring molds with aluminum foil, lightly oil the inside of the rings, and place on a sheet pan. Pour in and swirl around just enough of the caramelized sugar to cover the bottom of each mold.

Blanch 4 of the peaches in boiling water for 10 seconds, then shock them in ice water. Remove the skin in strips and set the strips aside (reserve the peach flesh for another use). Cut the remaining 4 peaches into ¼-inch-thick round slices. Press a sliced peach in the ring mold on top of the caramelized sugar and refrigerate for 5 minutes. Spoon in the batter to fill the molds three-quarters of the way full. Bake at 350 degrees for 20 minutes, or until the cake springs back when pressed lightly in the center. Invert the cakes on the sheet pan while warm and remove the foil and the ring mold.

To make the candied peach skin: Cook the reserved peach skins with the remaining ½ cup water, 6 tablespoons of the sugar, and the lemon juice for 15 minutes over medium heat. Set aside in the syrup.

To make the almond sauce: Bring the cream and the remaining 1 tablespoon sugar to a boil. Remove from the heat, add the almonds, cover, and steep for 10 minutes. Purée for 2 minutes, or until smooth.

ASSEMBLY Spoon some of the almond sauce onto the center of each plate. Place a cake on the almond sauce and spoon some of the candied peach skin in front of the cake. Place a quenelle of Almond Sherbet on the peach skins and sprinkle the Candied Almonds around the plate.

Almond Sherbet

Yield: approximately 2 cups

1 cup milk

1 cup plus 2 tablespoons freshly squeezed orange juice

1½ cups toasted, ground almonds

6 tablespoons corn syrup

½ cup Simple Syrup (see Appendices)

METHOD Purée the milk, orange juice, and nuts for 2 minutes, or until smooth. Strain through a fine-mesh sieve and add the corn syrup and Simple Syrup. Refrigerate to chill and then freeze in an ice cream machine. Keep frozen until ready to use.

Candied Almonds

Yield: 1 cup

1 tablespoon corn syrup

Pulp of ½ vanilla bean

1 teaspoon Simple Syrup (see Appendices)

1 cup sliced almonds

METHOD Mix together the corn syrup, vanilla, and Simple Syrup. Toss the syrup mixture with the nuts and spread on a non-stick sheet pan. Bake at 350 degrees for 6 to 7 minutes, or until the nuts are golden brown. Remove from the oven, let cool, and store in an airtight container at room temperature.

Maytag Blue Cheese Brioche Tart with Black Corinth Grapes

The special elegance of this dessert stems from the fact that it is not overly sweet.
It's like a cheese course that is just barely pushed into dessert territory. The brioche is
soft and buttery and the Corinth grapes are plump and possess an almost tangy sweetness.
The blue cheese is just melted and asserts its poignant flavor without taking over. Finally,
a playful sweet-tart sauce is spooned around the edges of the tart to provide a little fruity moisture.
This tart can either be served right out of the oven or made a few hours ahead and reheated.

Serves 6

Brioche Dough (see Appendices)
½ cup crème fraîche
1 egg yolk
½ cup Maytag blue cheese
1½ cups Black Corinth grapes
1 egg, beaten
¼ cup plus 1 tablespoon sugar
2 tablespoons water

METHOD To make the tarts: Refrigerate the Brioche Dough for at least 3 hours. Roll the dough out to ⅛ inch thick and cut into six 5-inch circles. Fold about ½ inch of the edges toward the center, twisting and pinching the dough to form a finished edge. Press the brioche circles into 3-inch-diameter by ½-inch-high tart rings, cover with plastic wrap, and set in a warm place to rise for 45 minutes.

Thoroughly mix the crème fraîche with the 1 egg yolk. Press down the dough in the bottom of the tarts and evenly distribute the blue cheese and ½ cup of the grapes into the tarts. Place a spoonful of the crème fraîche mixture into the tarts, brush the top of the dough lining the perimeter of the mold with the egg, and sprinkle about ½ teaspoon of the sugar over the top of each one. Bake at 350 degrees for 20 to 30 minutes, or until golden brown.

To make the sauce: Cook the remaining ¼ cup sugar and the water in a heavy-bottomed sauté pan over medium heat for 5 minutes, or until golden brown. Add the remaining grapes and remove from the heat. If the sugar seizes, warm again over low heat until it is melted.

ASSEMBLY Place a tart in the center of each plate and spoon the grape sauce around the tarts.

Baked Pear with Blue Cheese Fondant and Pine Nut Baklava

This is sort of a half dessert, half cheese course. It's not too sweet, and the cheese element is utterly enveloping in its sensuality. The honeyed pine nuts in the crispy baklava excite the palate and accentuate the pungency of the cheese. Apple could be substituted for the pear for an interesting flavor variation.

Serves 8

4 Bosc pears, halved, with skin and stems

³/₄ cup Simple Syrup (see Appendices)

6 tablespoons Château d'Yquem

³/₄ cup heavy cream

4 ounces crumbled blue cheese

1 tablespoon black pepper, plus additional, to taste

¹/₄ cup mascarpone

¹/₂ cup pine nuts, toasted

2 tablespoons unsalted butter

2 tablespoons sugar

1 teaspoon cinnamon

Pine Nut Baklava (recipe follows)

METHOD To make the pears: Core the pears and scoop out some of the surrounding flesh to make a cavity. Combine ¹/₄ cup of the Simple Syrup and 2 tablespoons of the Chateau d'Yquem and brush it on the skin of the pears. Place the pears, cut side down, on a parchment-lined sheet pan and bake at 350 degrees for 45 minutes, or until tender, brushing with the syrup mixture every 15 minutes. Remove from the oven and let cool to room temperature.

To make the fondant: Whip the cream until it forms soft peaks. Add ¹/₄ cup of the blue cheese, the 1 tablespoon black pepper, and the mascarpone and whip until stiff peaks form. Fill the cavity of each pear half with the blue cheese mixture.

To make the candied pine nuts: Cook the pine nuts with the butter and sugar over medium heat for 5 minutes, or until the sugar is caramelized and the nuts are golden brown. Remove the nuts to a Silpat-lined or nonstick sheet pan, separating them. As they cool, break apart any nuts that stick together.

To make the sauce: Whisk together the remaining ¹/₂ cup Simple Syrup, the 4 tablespoons Château d'Yquem, and the cinnamon in a small saucepan over low heat to warm and combine.

ASSEMBLY Place a rectangle of Pine Nut Baklava toward the back of each plate. Place a pear half in the center of each plate with the top resting on the baklava. Drizzle some of the cinnamon sauce around the pear and sprinkle with the pine nuts. Sprinkle the remaining blue cheese on the pears and around the plates and grind a small amount of black pepper over each pear.

Pine Nut Baklava

Yield: 12 servings

2 cups pine nuts, toasted and chopped

¹/₂ cup unsalted butter, melted

1 cup honey

¹/₄ teaspoon ground cinnamon

¹/₈ teaspoon ground nutmeg

9 sheets filo dough

Confectioners' sugar, for dusting

¹/₂ cup finely ground pine nuts

¹/₂ cup Simple Syrup (see Appendices)

METHOD Combine the chopped pine nuts, ¹/₄ cup of the butter, the honey, cinnamon, and nutmeg in a small bowl. Lay 1 piece of filo on the work surface, brush with butter, and dust with confectioners' sugar and 1 tablespoon of the ground pine nuts. Cover with another filo sheet, brush with butter, and dust with confectioners' sugar and more pine nuts. Top this layer with a filo sheet, brush with butter, and set aside. Repeat this process with the remaining sheets of filo, making 3 stacks of 3 filo sheets. Cut the filo stacks in half and then cut each piece to fit an 8 by 8-inch or a 9 by 9-inch pan. Place one of the stacks in the pan and spread some of the honey-nut mixture on the filo. Top with another filo stack and continue the layering, ending with a layer of filo. Cover with plastic wrap and refrigerate for 1 hour.

Place the Simple Syrup in a small saucepan over medium-low heat and cook for 10 minutes, or until reduced by half. Brush half of the mixture on top of the baklava and bake at 350 degrees for 30 to 40 minutes, or until golden brown. Pour the remaining Simple Syrup over the top, let cool, and then cut into 1 by 3-inch rectangles.

Appendices

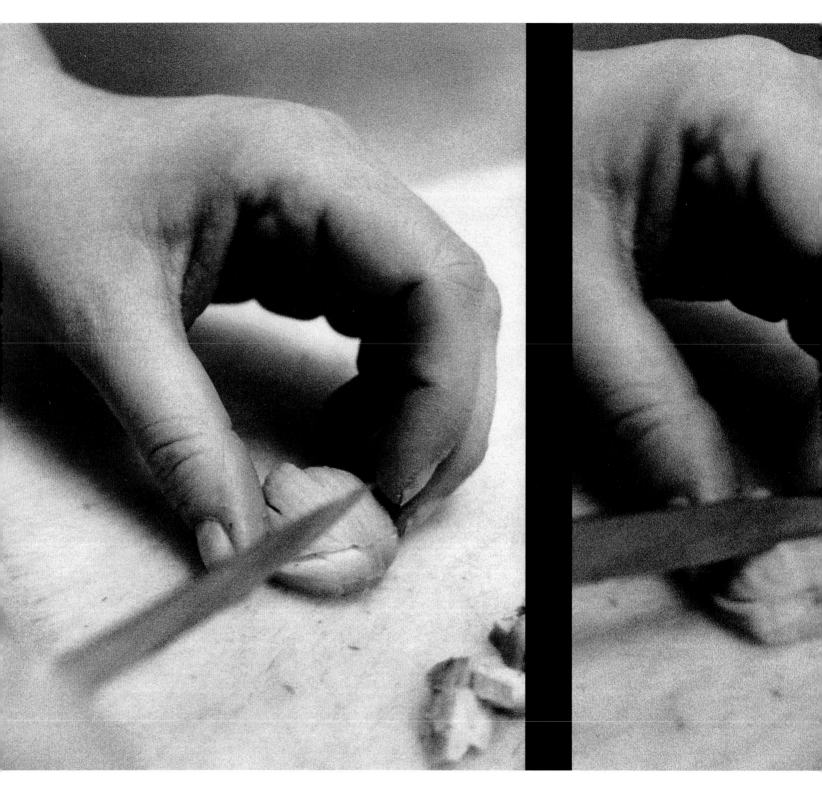

Recipes at a Glance

Basic Recipes

Brioche Dough

Yield: one 9 by 4-inch loaf

1/4 cup milk, warmed
2 teaspoons active dry yeast
1/2 cup plus 3 1/2 tablespoons all-purpose flour
1 1/2 cups plus 3 tablespoons high-gluten flour
2 tablespoons plus 1/2 teaspoon sugar
1 teaspoon salt
2 eggs
3/4 cup unsalted butter, at room temperature

METHOD Pour the milk over the yeast in a small bowl and let sit for several minutes. Stir to dissolve the yeast. Combine the flours, sugar, and salt in a large mixing bowl, add the milk and eggs, and mix in an electric mixer fitted with a dough hook on low speed until the dough comes together. Add the butter and continue to mix for 25 to 30 minutes, scraping occasionally, or until the dough is smooth and pulls away from the sides of the bowl.

Chocolate Sauce

Yield: 1/2 cup

2 tablespoons heavy cream
1 tablespoon unsalted butter
2 ounces bittersweet chocolate, chopped

METHOD Bring the cream to a boil and immediately pour it over the butter and chocolate. Stir until smooth.

Chocolate Sorbet

Yield: approximately 3 cups

2 cups water
1/4 cup unsweetened cocoa
1/2 cup sugar
4 ounces bittersweet chocolate, chopped
1 tablespoon corn syrup
1 cup freshly squeezed orange juice

METHOD Bring the water, cocoa, and sugar to a boil, pour over the chocolate, and stir until the chocolate is completely melted. Add the corn syrup and orange juice and mix well. Refrigerate to chill and then freeze in an ice cream machine. Keep frozen until ready to use.

Clear Lady Apple Chips

Yield: 20 to 25 chips

2 cups water
1 cup sugar
1/4 cup freshly squeezed lemon juice
20 to 25 thin slices lady apples

METHOD Bring the water, sugar, and lemon juice to a simmer, add the apple slices, and simmer for 10 minutes, or until the slices are translucent. Remove the apple slices from the liquid and lay them flat on a Silpat-lined sheet pan. Bake at 225 degrees for 1 hour, or until the apples are thoroughly dry. Carefully transfer the chips to a cooling rack. Store in an airtight container at room temperature until ready to use.

Cream Cheese Dough

Yield: one 9-inch piecrust

4 ounces cream cheese, cold, cut in chunks
4 ounces unsalted butter, cold, cut in chunks
4 ounces flour

METHOD Mix the cream cheese, butter, and flour until it just comes together. (There should still be streaks of cream cheese.) Remove the dough from the bowl, pat into a disk, cover with plastic wrap, and refrigerate for at least 1 hour before use.

Filo Bases

3 sheets filo dough
1/4 cup unsalted butter, melted
Confectioners' sugar, for dusting

METHOD Lay out a sheet of filo on the work surface, brush with one-third of the butter, and sprinkle with confectioners' sugar. Top with another sheet of filo, brush with another third of the butter, and sprinkle with confectioners' sugar. Top with the remaining filo sheet and brush with the remaining butter. For the filo rectangles, cut at least six 2 1/4 by 1 3/4-inch rectangles, place on a sheet pan, and cover with parchment. Place a sheet pan on top of the parchment, weight it down with a brick or other heavy, ovenproof object, and bake at 325 degrees for 10 minutes, or until golden brown. For the filo circles, cut at least six 1/4-inch-wide by 4-inch-long strips from the remaining filo. Bend the strips into circles and pinch the ends tightly to seal. Place on a sheet pan and bake at 325 degrees for 5 to 10 minutes, or until browned.

Honey-Chickpea Ice Cream

Yield: approximately 3 cups

2 cups heavy cream
1/2 cup cooked chickpeas
2 tablespoons orange zest
1/4 cup honey
4 egg yolks

METHOD Bring the cream, chickpeas, and orange zest to a boil. Remove from heat, cover, and steep for 30 minutes. Prepare an ice water bath. Purée the mixture and return to a boil. Combine the honey and egg yolks in a small bowl and slowly pour in some of the hot cream to temper the eggs. Pour the eggs into the cream mixture and continue cooking over low heat for 2 to 3 minutes, or until the mixture coats the back of a spoon and steam begins to rise from the top. Strain through a fine-mesh sieve. Cool over the ice water bath, stirring occasionally, until chilled. Pour into an 8 by 8-inch or 9 by 9-inch plastic wrap–lined pan and freeze for at least 1 hour. Cut into 3-inch squares just prior to serving.

Milk Chocolate Ice Cream

Yield: 3 cups

1 1/2 cups heavy cream
1/2 cup milk
4 egg yolks
1/4 cup sugar
2 ounces milk chocolate, chopped

METHOD Prepare an ice water bath. Bring the cream and milk to a boil. Whisk together the yolks and sugar and slowly pour in some of the hot cream to temper the yolks. Pour the eggs into the cream mixture and cook for 2 or 3 minutes, or until the mixture coats the back of a spoon and steam rises from the top. Strain the cream over the chopped chocolate and whisk until the chocolate is completely melted. Cool over the ice water bath, stirring occasionally, until the mixture is chilled. Freeze in an ice cream machine and keep frozen until ready to use.

Mint Syrup

Yield: approximately 1/3 cup

1/2 cup fresh mint leaves
1/4 cup fresh spinach leaves
1/4 cup Simple Syrup (see Appendices)
1 tablespoon oil

METHOD Blanch the mint and spinach in boiling water for 10 seconds, remove from the pan, and immediately shock in ice water. Squeeze out the excess water and coarsely chop. Purée with the Simple Syrup and oil for 3 minutes and strain through a fine-mesh sieve. Refrigerate until needed.

Nut/Seed Praline

Yield: 1 cup

1/2 cup sugar
1/4 cup water
1/2 cup hickory nuts, almonds, black walnuts, pine nuts, pumpkin seeds, pecans, peanuts, or macadamias

METHOD In a medium, heavy-bottomed sauté pan, combine the sugar and water over medium heat and cook for 10 minutes, or until golden brown. Swirl the pan as necessary to distribute the caramel. Stir in the nuts. If any of the sugar crystallizes, continue to cook over low heat to remelt. Pour the nuts and caramel onto a lightly oiled nonstick sheet pan. Let cool and then coarsely chop. (For individual "pralined" nuts, remove the nuts from the sugar individually with a fork and set them on a sheet pan to cool.) Store the praline in an airtight container at room temperature until ready to use.

Oven-Dried Strawberry Chips

Yield: approximately 1/4 cup

10 strawberries
2 to 3 teaspoons sugar

METHOD Slice the strawberries about 1/8 inch thick and lay them on a Silpat-lined or nonstick sheet pan. Sprinkle the slices with the sugar and bake at 225 degrees for 1 hour, or until the strawberries are dry. Remove the chips from the pan while warm. Let cool and then coarsely chop.

Poached Rhubarb Strips

Yield: 1/4 cup

1/2 cup Simple Syrup (see Appendices)
1/4 cup finely julienned rhubarb

METHOD Bring the Simple Syrup to a boil. Drop the rhubarb strips into the syrup for 10 seconds and remove them from the pan with a slotted spoon.

Preserved Ginger

Yield: 1/2 cup

1/2 cup julienned fresh ginger
1/2 cup sugar
1 cup water

METHOD Blanch the ginger in boiling water for 10 seconds. Drain and blanch in boiling water 2 more times. Bring the sugar and water to a boil, add the ginger, and simmer for 20 minutes. Refrigerate in the syrup until ready to use.

Simple Syrup

Yield: approximately 3 cups

2 cups water
2 cups sugar

METHOD Bring the water and sugar to a boil, remove from the heat, and let cool. The syrup may be kept for up to 1 month in the refrigerator.

Variation: For Vanilla Simple Syrup, add the pulp and pod of 1/2 vanilla bean to the sugar and water and proceed as directed for Simple Syrup.

Vanilla Tuile Batter

Yield: 2 cups

6 tablespoons unsalted butter
Pulp and pod of 1/2 vanilla bean
3 egg whites
1/2 cup plus 1 tablespoon sugar
1/2 cup plus 1 tablespoon flour

METHOD Melt the butter with the vanilla pulp and bean and remove from the heat as soon as the butter melts. Discard the vanilla bean and let the vanilla butter cool. Whisk the egg whites until they are frothy. Gradually pour in the sugar and then beat until soft peaks form. Mix in the cooled butter and fold in the flour until just combined. Refrigerate for up to 1 week.

Dessert Terms

BARBADOS CHERRIES A bright red fruit that grows wild in tropical climates. It looks like a ribbed cherry and has a floraly red currant flavor.

BATON (bâtonette) A cut the size of a wooden matchstick ($\frac{1}{8}$ by $\frac{1}{8}$ by 2 inches)

BLACK CORINTH GRAPES Very tiny delicate purple-red grape clusters. These sweet grapes have no seeds and thin skins. They are temperature sensitive and must be kept cool once picked.

BLANCH AND SHOCK To plunge a food into boiling salted water briefly and then immediately place it in ice water to stop the cooking process. This method is often used to firm the flesh or loosen the skin of fruits such as peaches or tomatoes. It is also used to heighten and set the color and flavor of herbs and greens.

BONIATO A white sweet potato that is a staple in Vietnam and Mexico.

BUDDHA'S HAND FRUIT A large, misshapen citrus fruit with fingerlike protrusions around the sides of the fruit. It has a yellow-green skin and a bitter fruit that is usually poached or candied to remove the bitterness.

CARAMBOLA (also called starfruit) A waxy, yellow, five-sided fruit with edible skin. Its flavor can range from exotically to refreshingly tart. Generally, the broader set the ribs, the sweeter the fruit.

CARAMELIZE To heat sugar until it liquefies and becomes a golden brown syrup. This can be done to varying degrees of darkness depending on the intensity of the desired flavor.

CONFIT Fruit cooked in its natural juices, with the addition of Simple Syrup to ensure that no flavor is lost during the cooking process.

CRÈME FRAÎCHE A true crème fraîche is an unpasteurized, 30 percent cream that has been allowed to ferment and thicken naturally. It has a nutty, faintly sour flavor and a velvety rich texture. In the United States, (where all commercial dairy products are pasteurized), crème fraîche is made with whipping cream and buttermilk. To make your own, use $\frac{1}{2}$ cup whipping cream and 1 tablespoon buttermilk, cover, and let sit at room temperature for 8 to 24 hours, or until very thick. Stir well and store in the refrigerator for up to 10 days. Do not substitute sour cream in recipes.

CUBAN BANANAS Small, red-skinned bananas with a slightly creamier texture and more tart taste than regular bananas.

CURRANTS Tiny berries related to the gooseberry. They come in black, red, or the more unusual white currant. They are often used for preserves or syrups, but they are also good to eat fresh.

DEGLAZE When foods have been sautéed or roasted, the coagulated juices collect in the pan. Deglazing is the process of adding liquid to the pan and dissolving these flavorful deposits over heat.

DOUBLE BOILER A cooking method in which a metal bowl or pot is placed over a larger pot of barely simmering water. You must have a tight fit between the bowl and the pot to keep any steam from escaping. This process is used for slowly cooking delicate items such as eggs, stovetop custards, or for melting chocolate.

EMULSION A sauce that is formed when one substance is suspended in another rather than fully combined. Emulsions are particularly fragile because they are not a true mixture—if they are not handled properly, they can separate or break.

ENNIS HAZELNUTS Organic hazelnuts from Trufflebert Farm in Oregon.

FILO Tissue-thin layers of pastry dough used in various Greek and Near East sweet and savory preparations. It is packaged fresh and frozen.

FORELLE PEARS Small, bell-shaped pears with crimson-speckled, yellow skin and sweet, juicy flesh.

FRENCH MELON A melon the size of a large orange that is very similar to a cantaloupe.

FRAISES DES BOIS Intensely sweet, tiny wild strawberries from France that come in red and white varieties. They are very delicate and bruise easily.

GELATIN Available in two forms—sheet or powdered. The more commonly available is the powdered form. To substitute powdered gelatin for sheet gelatin, replace $1\frac{1}{2}$ teaspoons powdered gelatin for one sheet gelatin. Dissolve the powdered gelatin in $1\frac{1}{2}$ tablespoons of cool water and proceed with the recipe.

HOJA SANTA A Mexican plant that grows in the wild. The leaves have a star-anise or licorice flavor.

HOKKAIDO A small, oval, dark-green skinned Japanese squash with bright orange sweet-pumpkin-flavored flesh.

HORNED MELON A bright yellow, spike-covered fruit with juicy green flesh. It is most often juiced to avoid the abundance of seeds throughout the flesh.

ICE WATER BATH The process of cooling down a hot liquid such as an ice cream or sorbet base in a bowl immersed in a second bowl filled with ice and water. The ice bath not only rapidly cools the liquid without direct contact with the ice water, but it stops the cooking process so the eggs in the ice cream base do not curdle.

ISRAELI COUSCOUS (MIDDLE EASTERN COUSCOUS) A larger grain of semolina, first manufactured in Israel and currently manufactured throughout the Middle East. It should be rinsed before and after cooking. It takes longer to cook than regular couscous.

LEMONGRASS A scented grass used as an herb in Southeast Asian cooking. Although the whole stalk may be used, usually the outer leaves are removed and only the bottom third of the stalk is used. Has a lemon-strawlike flavor.

MANDOLINE A kitchen tool that is efficient in cutting fruits and vegetables into precise cuts or slices, such as a julienne or a baton.

OFFSET SPATULA An inverted pallet knife used for icing cakes and for transferring or removing food products, available in a variety of sizes.

PARCHMENT PAPER A heavy, grease- and moisture-resistant paper that is often used to line baking sheets. Its many other uses include making disposable pastry bags.

PARISIENNE BALL A small round ball ranging from $\frac{1}{8}$ to $\frac{1}{4}$ inch in diameter.

POACHING To cook food gently in liquid at or just below the boiling point.

QUENELLE Traditionally, an oval dumpling made of forcemeat (very finely ground meats). In modern cooking, "quenelle" refers to a shape, not an ingredient. It's often made with ice cream, sorbet, or other semisoft foods and can be formed easily with one or two spoons.

RIBBON STAGE A stage in mixing when the whisk or beater can be lifted out of the mixture and the mixture falls slowly back onto the surface, forming a ribbonlike pattern. Another way to test for proper consistency is to draw a line in the mixture with your finger—if the line stays for a few seconds, you have reached ribbon stage.

SAPOTE This tropical fruit has a creamy, custardlike flesh. There are several different varieties: White sapote is orange-sized with bright green to canary yellow skin and a pale cream colored flesh. Mamey sapote is football-shaped with rough brown skin and bright salmon colored flesh. Chico sapote is oval-shaped with brown skin and medium brown flesh. Black sapote is dark green-skinned with flesh the color of chocolate pudding.

SILPAT A flexible, ovenproof, nonstick silicone baking sheet. Water- and moisture-repellent, it can be placed in oven temperatures up to 600 degrees. These pan liners are great for drying fruits, making tuiles, and for sugar and tempered chocolate work.

TEMPER To slowly add hot liquid to a cold substance while continuously whisking until the cold liquid is warm. This is often done in ice cream and custard preparations to prevent the egg yolks from curdling.

TEMPERED CHOCOLATE Chocolate that has been heated to 110 to 115 degrees, cooled to 80 degrees, then reheated to 84 to 86 degrees. Tempering chocolate results in a harder, glossier finish.

TEMPLATE A stencil cut out of a thin sheet of plastic or coated cardboard used to create precise shapes such as a square, circle, or triangle. Usually used when multiple pieces are needed.

TERRINE The word "terrine" is used to describe both a mold and the food that has been prepared in the mold. Terrine molds come in many shapes, but they are most commonly rectangular with removable sides (so the food can be removed from the mold without damaging its shape). For the recipes in this book, the terrine need not be ovenproof. All of the terrines in this book are made in 2¼ by 1½ by 8-inch molds that can be purchased through Charlie Trotter's.

TUILE Thin, crispy wafers that are often molded around a curved surface immediately after they come out of the oven, which gives them a shape resembling a curved tile (tuile in French). They can also be prepared as flat disks and used for layering foods.

UGLI FRUIT A large, juicy citrus fruit with thick, puffy, semiloose skin that can be slightly bumpy. Their flavor suggests grapefruit with hints of mandarin.

WATER BATH A pan of water into which a smaller pan is set to cook. It is often used with custards and other egg preparations to evenly cook the eggs and prevent curdling.

Weights & Measures

Ounces to grams: multiply by 28.35

Teaspoons to milliliters: multiply by 5

Tablespoons to milliliters: multiply by 15

Fluid ounces to milliliters: multiply by 30

Cups to liters: multiply by .24

Fahrenheit to Celsius: subtract 32, multiply by 5, and divide by 9

Ingredient	Unit	Volume			Weight	
		Teaspoon	Tablespoon	Cup	Ounces	Grams
Baking powder		1 teaspoon				5 grams
Baking soda		1 teaspoon				5 grams
Butter				1 cup	8 ounces	227 grams
Chocolate				1 cup	6 ounces	170 grams
Citrus zest		1 teaspoon				2 grams
Cocoa				1 cup	3 ounces	84 grams
Corn syrup				1 cup	11.5 ounces	328 grams
Cornstarch			1 tablespoon		.25 ounce	7 grams
Cream cheese				1 cup	8 ounces	227 grams
Cream, heavy				1 cup	8.12 ounces	232 grams
Cream of tartar		1 teaspoon				3.1 grams
Eggs (no shell)	1 large		3½ tablespoons plus ½ teaspoon		1.75 ounces	50 grams
Egg whites	1 large		2 tablespoons		1 ounce	30 grams
Egg yolks	1 large	3½ teaspoons			.65 ounce	19 grams
Flour, all-purpose				1 cup	5 ounces	145 grams
Flour, bread				1 cup	5.5 ounces	157 grams
Flour, cake				1 cup	4.5 ounces	130 grams
Flour, whole wheat				1 cup	5.75 ounces	165 grams
Gelatin	1 sheet	1½ teaspoons				4.7 grams
Honey				1 cup	11.75 ounces	336 grams
Lemon juice				1 cup	8.75 ounces	250 grams
Milk				1 cup	8.5 ounces	242 grams
Molasses				1 cup	11.25 ounces	322 grams
Oil				1 cup	7.5 ounces	215 grams
Orange juice				1 cup	8.5 ounces	242 grams
Poppyseeds				¼ cup	1.25 ounces	36 grams
Salt		1 teaspoon				7 grams
Sour cream				1 cup	8.5 ounces	242 grams
Sugar				1 cup	7 ounces	200 grams
Sugar, brown				1 cup	7.66 ounces	217 grams
Sugar, confectioners'				1 cup	4 ounces	115 grams
Vanilla extract		1 teaspoon				4 grams
Water				1 cup	8.34 ounces	236 grams

Index

Ten Speed Press
Box 7123
Berkeley, California 94710
www.tenspeed.com

Distributed in Australia by Simon and Schuster Australia,
in Canada by Ten Speed Press Canada,
in New Zealand by Southern Publishers Group,
in South Africa by Real Books, and
in the United Kingdom and Europe by Airlift Book Company.

Project Coordinator and General Editor: Judi Carle, Charlie Trotter's
Editor: Lorena Jones, Ten Speed Press
Copyeditor: Suzanne Sherman
Research, development, and recipe testing:
Sari Zernich, Charlie Trotter's

Typeset in Monotype Walbaum by Paul Baker Typography, Inc., Chicago

Library of Congress Cataloging-in-Publication Data

Trotter, Charlie.
Charlie Trotter's desserts / recipes by Charlie Trotter & Michelle Gayer;
color photography by Tim Turner; black & white photography by Paul Elledge.
p.   cm.
Includes index.
ISBN 0-89815-815-X (alk. paper)

1. Desserts 2. Charlie Trotter's (Restaurant)
I. Gayer, Michelle. II. Title.
TX773.T76 1998
641.8'6—dc21   96-24526
                                                    CIP

Printed in China by C&C Offset Printing Co., Ltd
First printing, 1998

2 3 4 5 6 7 8 9 10 — 08 07 06 05 04